The Tahoe Rim Trail:
A Complete Guide
For Hikers, Mountain
Bikers, and Equestrians

(Top) Sand Harbor overlook, Lake Tahoe Nevada State Park.

(Bottom) Lower Echo Lake.

The Tahoe Rim Trail: A Complete Guide

For Hikers, Mountain Bikers, and Equestrians

ENDORSED BY
THE TAHOE RIM
TRAIL ASSOCIATION

by Tim Hauserman

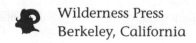
Wilderness Press
Berkeley, California

FIRST EDITION June 2002
Second printing October 2002
Third printing April 2003
Fourth printing August 2003

All photographs by the author unless otherwise indicated.
Front cover photo by Mark Vollmer, "*Sierra Soda Straws* frame view from
    south ridge of Martis Peak"
Frontispiece photos by Mark Vollmer
Maps by Tom Harrison, using mapping
    information from Jeffrey P. Schaffer
Cover design by Jaan Hitt
Book design and composition by Scott Perry, Archetype Typography

Library of Congress Card Catalog Number: 2002023450
ISBN 0-89997-288-8
UPC 7-19609-97288-4

Published by Wilderness Press
        1200 5th Street
        Berkeley, CA 94710
        Toll-free: (800) 443-7227
        Fax: (510) 558-1696

        info@wildernesspress.com
        www.wildernesspress.com
        Contact us for a free catalog

Library of Congress Cataloging-in-Publication Data
Hauserman, Tim, 1958-
    The Tahoe Rim Trail : a complete guide / by Tim Hauserman.
    --1st ed.
        p. cm.
    "Endorsed by the Tahoe Rim Trail Association."
    Includes bibliographical references and index.
    ISBN 0-89997-288-8
    1. Hiking--Tahoe Rim Trail (Calif. and Nev.)--Guidebooks. 2. All-
terrain cycling--Tahoe Rim Trail (Calif. and Nev.)--Guidebooks.
3. Horsemanship--Tahoe Rim Trail (Calif. and Nev.)--Guidebooks.
4. Tahoe Rim Trail (Calif. and Nev.)--Guidebooks. I. Tahoe Rim Trail
Association. II. Title.

GV199.42.T18H38 2002
917.94'38--dc21
                                                    2002023450

Acknowledgements

First of all, I want to thank Mother Nature, whose handiwork in creating Lake Tahoe so impressed me with its beauty that I could not stay away. This book is the result of all the joy I have felt in the woods and meadows around Lake Tahoe.

The Tahoe Rim Trail Association has been supportive along the way, especially Associate Director Shannon Raborn, who heard me say too many times, "Could you read through this and let me know what you think?" Sara Holm, who had the joy of reading it at different stages, let me know when it was improving. Thanks to all TRTA Board Members who also read sections of the book to make sure I was on the right track; these include Max Jones, Jay Abdo, Jennifer Hogler, Jim Backhus, Shirley Moore and others. Lynda McDowell, Executive Director of the Tahoe Rim Trail has also been supportive.

Thanks to Robert McDowell, David Allessio, and Lori Allessio at the Forest Service for many excellent suggestions. Shelly Segale and Karen Honeywell reviewed the manuscript and also contributed useful comments. Susie Denison wrote a terrific local book, *The Dog Lover's Guide to Lake Tahoe*, and convinced me that I could write this one. She told me it would not be easy. She was right.

Thanks to my buddies who hiked and biked with me and put up with my blabbing into a tape recorder: Jan Corda, Monika Klecka (the over-the-bars champ), Bud Tremayne, Shannon Raborn, Toni Blair, Laurie Buffington, and Karen Schwartz (who also did the great drawing on page 42). The

Tahoe Rim Trail 150-Mile Club encouraged me to hike the trail the first time, which made it easier the second and the third. Tahoe Trips and Trails gave me the occasional thrill of getting paid to hike; they've got a great manual on animals and plants at Lake Tahoe. I am very appreciative that I have been allowed to use the wonderful animal print drawings by Jessica Land, a fellow guide at Tahoe Trips and Trails. Rick Galleen let me look through all the trail information that he has collected.

Thanks to Glenn Hampton for starting the trail in the first place. Tom Harrison's dog-eared map went with me on all my hikes and I thank him for creating the maps in this book. Thanks to all the great horse folks including Sonya Willits whose cogent letter summarized the horse issue for me, and to Clayton Myers, Bob Stevens, and Jim Larimer for their information on horseback riding on the Rim Trail. My helpful fishing sources included Jerome Yesavage, Bruce Ajari, and Ralph Cutter. Anne Bryant from the Bear Preservation League reviewed my bear information and was a great source on squirrels.

Besides providing information and assistance, Jeffrey P. Schaffer, another Wilderness Press author, read and reviewed the manuscript in detail and contributed to the wonderful maps in the book. His reputation for meticulous mapping and guidebook authoring skills is well deserved. Thanks to Mark Vollmer for his support and the beautiful front and back cover photos. Keep your eyes open for his "coffee table" photo book on the Rim Trail that he hopes to complete in the next few years.

My wife, Sandy, and daughters, Sarah and Hannah, had to hear too many times, "Sorry I can't make it, I will be out hiking that day." Thanks to local Tahoe City merchants like The Back Country and Alpenglow who told me the book would sell.

Wilderness Press had faith in me. I still remember the first message on my voice mail: "We will do your book, but it will need a lot of editing." Yes, as my editor Jannie Dresser can attest, those words were oh so true. Speaking of Jannie, she stuck with me valiantly through many drafts, guiding the text to be as good as it could be.

Heads Up!

Adventure in wilderness areas or mountain backcountry includes potential risks that you should be aware of and respect. The fact that a trail is described in this book is not a representation that it will be safe. Trails and trail conditions vary greatly in difficulty and in the degree of conditioning and agility one needs to enjoy them safely, whether you are hiking, backpacking, mountain biking, horseback riding, or in any other way using the trail for recreational purposes.

Routes may have changed or conditions may have deteriorated since the descriptions were written. Due to changes in weather, or in events related to storms, snowpack, and fire, trail conditions can vary from season to season, day to day, and hour to hour. A trail that is safe on a dry day may be unsafe under adverse weather conditions; a trail that is accessible to a prepared, agile, and properly equipped user, may be completely unsafe for a lesser skilled trail user or for someone with expertise who chooses to use a trail when conditions are unpredictable.

Minimize your risks by being knowledgeable, prepared and alert. There are a number of good books and public courses on trail safety, backpacking, physical fitness, and mountain survival and you should take advantage of them. Be aware of your own limitations and of conditions existing when and where you are hiking. If conditions are dangerous, or if you are not prepared to deal with them safely, choose a different hike! It is better to have wasted a drive than to be the subject of a mountain rescue.

These warnings are not intended to scare you off the trails. Millions of people have safe and enjoyable experiences in the outdoors every year. However, one element of the beauty, freedom and excitement of the wilderness is the presence of risks that you must assume when you hike, backpack, snowshoe, cross-country ski, horseback ride, mountain bike, or in any other way use the backcountry for recreational purposes. These risks can be met safely, but only when you exercise your good judgment and common sense.

Table of Contents

Foreword

As a cool dawn breaks high atop Mt. Tallac, I find myself completely spellbound by the spectacular awe-inspiring panarama before me. And my Impossible Dream of a trail completely around Lake Tahoe on the highest and most prominent mountain slopes suddenly takes shape.

Imagine a trail that winds completely around the most spectacular lake in the United States. As you hike along the 165-mile loop, you meander through areas rich in history. The trail leads you through old Washoe hunting grounds and long-vanished game trails, as well as trails made by early settlers fresh from obtaining their provisions at Genoa. Here, over 100 years ago, some of the West's first Basque sheepherders roamed through the mountain meadows with their flocks. You wade through waist-high grass, through magnificent stands of red fir and Jeffrey pine, and alongside cool mountain streams. You may journey high above mysterious places with names like "Hellhole" with its many pools and ground that shakes, rolls, and sways. At Grass Lake, you skirt the largest bog in the Sierra Nevada Mountain Range while most of the time you can view the highest and largest alpine lake in North America, Lake Tahoe. On the horizon, you can make out the Pine Nut Range in Nevada, the Sierra of California and the Carson Valley. You travel through six counties, three National Forests, and two states. A week and a half later, you're back where you started. This was the dream that inspired the Tahoe Rim Trail nearly twenty years ago.

Today, thanks to over 10,000 volunteers who worked tirelessly for over 18 years, the Tahoe Rim Trail has become a reality. In September of 2001, it officially opened with a ceremony that marked the completion of the last section of the trail. Now, you can enjoy this challenging trail by using Tim Hauserman's excellent guide with its concise and accurate descriptions of the fascinating vegetation that blankets the area. You will also be introduced to the many animals you may encounter along the trail. The maps, produced by Tom Harrison, and mileage figures verified by Jeffrey P. Schaffer, will help you better plan a safe and enjoyable trip. This guide will fast become your constant companion on the trail.

Use this guide to increase your awareness for the proper use and respect for the resources of the Tahoe Basin, but also use it to fully enjoy our new national treasure, the Tahoe Rim Trail.

Glenn Hampton
Founder of the Tahoe Rim Trail
May 2002

Relief Map of Trail Terrain

TRUCKEE RIVER

MT ROSE

INCLINE VILLAGE

SLIDE MTN

SQUAW VALLEY

TAHOE CITY

WARD CR

SPOONER SUMMIT

BLACKWOOD CR

GLENBROOK

GENOA PEAK

MCKINNEY CR

HWY 89

EMERALD BAY

SOUTH LAKE TAHOE

HEAVENLY VALLEY

FREEL PEAK

FALLEN LEAF LAKE

MEYERS

LUTHER PASS

ECHO SUMMIT

HWY 88/89

HWY 50

1

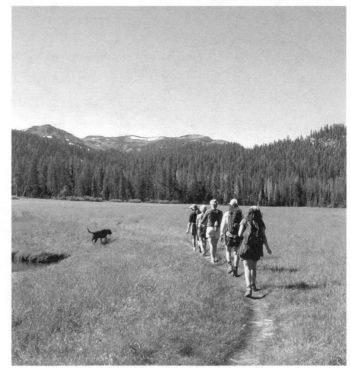

(Top)
View from
Christopher's
Loop looking
south.

(Bottom)
Hikers (and
dog) crossing
Big Meadow.

CHAPTER 1

Introduction to the Tahoe Area and Its New Trail

Then it seemed to me the Sierra should not be called the Nevada, or Snowy Range, but the Range of Light. And after ten years spent in the heart of it, rejoicing and wondering, bathing in its glorious floods of light, seeing the sunbursts of morning among the icy peaks, the noonday radiance on the trees and rocks and snow, the flush of the alpenglow, and a thousand dashing waterfalls with their marvelous abundance of irised spray, it still seems to be above all others the Range of Light, the most divinely beautiful of all the mountain chains I have ever seen.

—John Muir, 1912

Welcome to the Tahoe Rim Trail! This book will quickly and easily provide you with what you need to know in order to enjoy your time on this incredibly beautiful route. Having lived at Lake Tahoe most of my life, I've spent countless hours on area trails. While I am not a biologist, a geologist, a naturalist, or an "ist" of any kind, I have learned enough about Tahoe plants, animals, and mountains to deepen my interest when I am in the woods. I'd like to help make your outdoor experience just as fun and fascinating.

An enormous, deep-blue, subalpine lake surrounded by lofty, snowcapped peaks. Lush, green forests, dark volcanic peaks, stark granite faces and hundreds of small, jewel-like lakes adorning the wilderness areas above this special lake. Should someone build a loop trail here? Absolutely! In fact it is quite remarkable that the trail was completed only as recently as September 2001. If a loop trail should have been built anywhere in the world, this was the place.

The now 164-mile Tahoe Rim Trail circles one of the world's most beautiful lakes, and winds through two states, several wilderness areas, National Forest and state park lands, and an incredible diversity of geology, flora, and fauna. The trail accesses both the Sierra Nevada and its Carson Range spur, each with a unique personality. It winds through aspen meadows, skirts high mountain peaks, and runs for miles along ridgetops with stunning views. You can walk for miles under a forested canopy, or saunter through meadows. You can venture above treeline for long stretches. That the trail is a big loop, a circle, may be its best feature. Wherever you set off, as the days and weeks go by, you can follow the circle back to where you began. Across the big, blue expanse of the lake, you can pick out where you were a week ago, and where you will be again in another week. A multi-use path, much of the Tahoe Rim Trail was constructed for the pleasure of hikers, equestrians, and mountain bikers, using modern trail-building techniques, with the goal to not exceed an average grade of 10 percent.

Geographic Setting

Lake Tahoe is the largest subalpine lake in North America. At 22 miles long and 12 miles wide it is a beautiful expanse of deep, blue water. What

Lake Tahoe and its western mountains as seen from the east shore.

makes it so intensely blue? It's depth. At its deepest point Lake Tahoe plunges to 1645 feet with an average depth of approximately 900 feet. With its huge surface area, that's a lot of water. Tahoe is blue also because it is so clear and clean. The clarity is primarily due to the fact that the basin around the lake is fairly small, the water very cold, and the soils and vegetation have prevented nutrients from entering the lake where they increase algae growth.

Since the 1960s and 1970s there has been dramatic population growth and increased development in the Tahoe area. Development has had a negative impact on the lake. An increase in algae growth has reduced Tahoe's legendary clarity. A substantial investment of energy and money is now underway to protect the lake. For more information on how you can help, contact the League to Save Lake Tahoe at (530) 541-5388 or the Tahoe

Regional Planning Agency at (775) 588-4547. Call or write your Congressperson or Senator to ask for their support in efforts to clean up and protect this lake and its surroundings. You will find a handy list of "Ways to Save Lake Tahoe" at the end of this book.

Trail History

Glenn Hampton was a Recreation Officer for the Lake Tahoe Basin Management Unit of the United States Forest Service through the 1970s when he first had the idea of completing a trail with volunteer labor around the rim of Lake Tahoe. He forged a partnership between the Forest Service, the Nevada State Parks, and a newly created, not-for-profit volunteer organization called the Tahoe Rim Trail Fund. The purpose of the partnership was to plan, construct, and maintain a Tahoe Rim Trail. Since 1984 more than 100 miles of trail have been built or improved around the lake. The Tahoe Rim Trail also uses the existing Pacific Crest Trail in the section that overlaps from Meiss Meadows to Twin Peaks.

The Tahoe Rim Trail Fund (now known as the Tahoe Rim Trail Association) is administered by a volunteer Board of Directors and has a small professional staff. The trail has been built partially by professional crews hired by the Forest Service or Nevada State Parks, and partially by volunteers who have contributed thousands of hours. For many it has been a labor of love. Construction of the trail began in July 1984 from Grass Lake, on the north side of Highway 89 near Luther Pass, toward Kingsbury Grade. In 1985 two additional construction projects were started at Spooner Summit and Tahoe City. In 2001 the last section of the trail was completed, between Rose Knob Peak and Mount Baldy.

In 1999 former First Lady, Hillary Rodham Clinton, and the White House Millennium Council designated the Tahoe Rim Trail as the Millennium Trail for the State of Nevada. Bestowed on only one trail in each state, the Tahoe Rim Trail is certainly worthy of this honor and is destined to become one of the most popular trails in the United States, taking its place beside the Appalachian Trail, the Pacific Crest Trail, and the John Muir Trail.

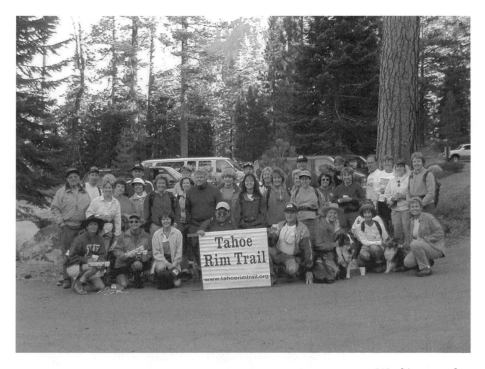

Working on the trail with the Tahoe Rim Trail Association.

The Tahoe Rim Trail Association

Funded through contributions, memberships, fundraising, and the sale of merchandise, the Tahoe Rim Trail Association has arranged for some 10,000 volunteers to work over 200,000 hours on the trail. The TRTA and their government partners have not only built or improved the trail, but they have also built two major trailhead facilities, and a

1.3-mile wheelchair-accessible interpretive trail. The TRTA is the prime information source for people interested in hiking, biking, or horseback riding on the Tahoe Rim Trail.

The TRTA also administers the Tahoe Rim Trail 165-Mile Club. Those who hike or bike (where allowed) the entire trail can become members of the Tahoe Rim Trail 165-Mile Club. An application form is available from the Tahoe Rim Trail Association.

The 165-Mile Club

The club was started before trail construction was completed and 150 miles was an original estimate of the trail's length. Once the trail was completed, it ended up being considerably longer. Tom Harrison and I calculate it to be 168.2 miles long, although most people will only hike the main sections of the trail which total nearly 165 miles. Thus, the name of the club was recently changed from the 150-Mile Club to the 165-Mile club.

Even though the Tahoe Rim Trail was completed in 2001, there is still much to do in order to maintain and improve the trail. Tasks include repairing damaged sections of the trail, as well as making changes to the trail to prevent future damage. Volunteers continue to add switchbacks, change routes, add connecting trails, and do whatever is necessary to improve the trail.

The Tahoe Rim Trail Association is key to the future of the trail and anyone can become a member. Members receive quarterly newsletters, an invitation to the annual meeting, discounts on merchandise, the opportunity to attend TRTA-led hikes, horseback rides, and bike rides, not to mention the satisfaction of knowing that they are doing their part for this wonderful trail. To obtain information contact :

Tahoe Rim Trail Association
DWR Community Non-Profit Center
948 Incline Way
Incline Village, NV 89451
(775) 298-0012
info@tahoerimtrail.org / www.tahoerimtrail.org

Regulations and Permits

The Tahoe Rim Trail travels through three National Forest Wilderness Areas: Mount Rose Wilderness, Desolation Wilderness, and Granite Chief Wilderness. Much of the rest of the trail is on National Forest lands in California and Nevada. The remainder of the trail lies in the Lake Tahoe Nevada State Park. The only areas with limitations on hiking or camping on the TRT are Desolation Wilderness and Lake Tahoe Nevada State Park. These include the following trail sections, described in greater detail in chapter 6.

Section 3: Tahoe Meadows to Spooner Summit. This section travels through Lake Tahoe Nevada State Park where camping is limited to two primitive but developed campgrounds which have picnic tables and pit toilets, but no water supplies. No permits are required here. For more information contact the Lake Tahoe Nevada State Park at (775) 831-0494 or the Tahoe Rim Trail Association office at (775) 298-0012.

Section 7: Echo Summit/Echo Lakes to Barker Pass. This section travels through Desolation Wilderness. Permits are required to enter Desolation Wilderness, and these permits can be obtained at the trailhead. If you are staying overnight, a camping permit must be obtained at the Tahoe Basin National Forest Information Center at Taylor Creek located on Highway 89 about 0.5 mile northwest of Camp Richardson. The wilderness has been divided

9

into zones for the issuance of permits. A limited number of camping permits are available for each zone, so the possibility exists of not being able to obtain a permit for the more popular areas (which tend to be lakes close to trailheads) in the middle of the summer, particularly on weekends. For more information contact the Forest Service at:

Lake Tahoe Basin Management Unit
870 Emerald Bay Road
South Lake Tahoe, CA 96150
(530) 573-2674

Cedar tree close to Tahoe City.

CHAPTER 2

Animals and Plants, Great and Small

The Lake Tahoe area has a tremendous variety of interesting flora and fauna.You will enhance your enjoyment and experience of this beautiful region by getting to know some of the animals and plants. This chapter gives a quick summary of what you may encounter as you journey along the Tahoe Rim Trail.

While many of these animals are a rare treat to encounter, the smaller animals such as squirrels and birds are found in abundance. Among the highlights of traveling in the Tahoe woods are the fascinating trees and wildflowers that you pass along the way. The descriptions of plants are designed to be simple to read and understand. This book provides a quick introduction to the most common animals and plants in the Tahoe Basin area; it is not intended to substitute for a good field guide. For those who want more information, several wildflower and plant field books are listed in the "Recommended Reading" section at the back of the book.

The Largest Animals in the Tahoe Region

Bear—The largest omnivores in the Sierra are black bears, but often their fur is cinnamon brown, dark

7 in

hind

front

BlackBear

brown, reddish and sometimes even off-white. Bears are common on the west shore of the lake, where numerous garbage cans provide a tempting place to scavenge a free meal on garbage collection days. Whether you live in the Tahoe area or are just visiting, you can do your part to protect bears—and yourself—by keeping your garbage away from where bears can get to it. If you are camping or backpacking in bear country, follow these simple rules:

❖ Don't leave any food or clothes that smell like food in your tent. When they come to get it, you don't want to be sleeping in the path of a hungry and determined bear.

❖ Put your food (all your food!) in a safe place at night and when you are not in camp. If a campground has a bearproof container use it. In the backcountry you are not only advised to put your food in a bearproof canister; in some areas, including several wilderness areas in the central and southern Sierra, you are required to do so. The next two best methods are to hang your food high in a tree, suspended from a rope, or to put it on a 15-foot-high rocky ledge where bears can't reach.

❖ Keep a clean camp so that bears or other animals won't be attracted to the site. Put food, cleaning and fragrant hygiene supplies such as shampoo, toothpaste, and soap away soon after you are done with them.

❖ If you see a bear, make lots of noise: bang pots and pans together, stand up and shout, and throw your arms around to scare the bear away. (Note: this doesn't always work!)

❖ Be smart. If a bear is chomping down on your food, it has already won, so don't try to take the food away from it.

❖ Never get between a mother bear and her cub.

❖ If you startle a bear, make eye contact, but do not stare at it. Instead, slowly back away and wait for the bear to amble off. Be sure to not block its escape route.

❖ Don't forget that bears are good runners *and* can climb trees.

❖ Treat bears with respect: remember, you are in their territory.

While it is important to be cautious, bear attacks are extremely rare. In those very unusual circumstances where bears have injured people, it was usually the result of human error. Be careful and enjoy bears from a safe distance.

Deer—The most common deer in the Sierra are named "mule deer" for their large, floppy ears that resemble those of a mule. Mule deer also sport a small white bob of a tail. Deep snow and lack of forage keep mule deer away from the area during winter months. At that time, you are more likely to find them in the warmer climes of the Carson Valley, a short jaunt over the Carson Range from the east shore. As the season warms up, these animals are commonly spotted on the east slopes and in other areas of the Tahoe basin.

Deer

Mountain Lion or Cougar—Known as either a mountain lion or cougar, the rare and elusive mountain lion has been seen occasionally in the Tahoe area, especially in lower elevation open areas such as the east shore and around Truckee. These large cats range in size between 6.5 to 8 feet long, including tail, and can weigh up to 200 pounds. Each animal has a vast range and can cover many miles of territory in one night. Mountain lions hunt deer primarily, although they also prey on raccoons, birds, mice, and even skunks and

Mountain Lion

13

porcupines. Porcupine?! That would have to be one hungry mountain lion.

Someone once brought a pet mountain lion to my office: its power and grace were awe-inspiring. You had the feeling that it could dispose of any one of us in half a minute. Mountain lions can jump 12 feet up a tree from a standstill position. If you do encounter one, experts warn not to run. Instead try to look as big as possible by standing tall, opening up your jacket, and waving your arms. Once the cat perceives that you don't behave like prey, it will probably back off. Also, a mountain lion leaves the remains of a kill and returns later to eat; needless to say, it is not wise to hang around a lion kill.

Medium-Sized Animals

Bobcat

Bobcat—You are more likely to hear this elusive member of the cat family with its loud scream or howl, than see it. With an average weight of about 20 pounds in adulthood, it is just a little larger than an average-sized domestic cat. A bobcat has a short stubby tail that is black toward the end and tipped with white. A nocturnal predator, the bobcat likes to dine on squirrels and mice. Bobcats have been rarely sighted in Tahoe Meadows and along the west shore.

Coyote

Coyote—These adaptable creatures are common in the Tahoe area. While I've seen them in many locations, they seem to prefer woodlands and meadows. They can often be heard yipping and howling at night in Ward and Blackwood canyons, Squaw Valley, Alpine Meadows, and other places. Though coyotes resemble medium-sized dogs, they are much more graceful and lissome when they run, a sight to behold. It is not uncommon for a dog to chase a single coyote, only to discover that the coyote is leading him back to his teammates. Although many believe that coyotes do not hunt in packs, I have seen them several times in groups of three or four adults. If you live in the mountains, take care with your domesticated animals, even around your home. Many a lost cat or small dog has become a coyote dinner.

Marten—It is a rare treat to spot a marten, also called pine marten. At about 1.5 to 3 feet long, including its tail, the marten is about the size of a housecat but longer and sleeker. Martens have beautiful lush brown fur and long bushy tails. They are agile climbers and sometimes live in a cavity high up in a tree. They are elusive animals, but can occasionally be seen in pursuit of squirrels or chipmunks, their favorite dinner. Several years ago we saw one in nearby trees around our Tahoe area house for about two weeks. The grace and stealth of the marten is unmatched.

Marmot

Marmot—If you hear a high-pitched squeak when you are walking by a big rock pile, there is a good chance that it harbors a yellow-bellied marmot. Also known as woodchuck or groundhog, the marmot is about the size of a housecat. Related to squirrels, marmots are dark brown and cinnamon in color, live in groups and love to sun themselves on rocks. I have often seen them in Desolation Wilderness, on the Pacific Crest Trail near Twin Peaks, and in the Mount Rose area.

Marmot.

Porcupine—These large rodents can often be seen on roads or sitting up in a tree. About 2 to 3 feet long, they are large and round with short legs. They have light brown to yellowish fur and numerous hollow but sharp quills of up to 3 inches long. The porcupine walks in a slow lumbering fashion—if no one wants to eat you, why hurry?—

15

and enjoys a diet of succulent bark and herbaceous plants. No animals, except cougars perhaps, want to have anything to do with these quill-covered critters, and although the quills *can* cause a great deal of pain, especially to over zealous dogs, it is a myth that they can "shoot" their quills.

Raccoon—These carnivorous little burglars are one of the most interesting animal species in the Sierra. The distinctive face looks like a burglar's mask, with a black band across the eyes and most of the face white. They range in size, but can get as big as a medium-sized dog. Raccoons are nocturnal, all the better to wake you in the middle of the night while they are knocking over garbage cans in pursuit of food. It is common to see them on house decks but rare to see them in the wild. Often the best evidence of a raccoon is the very distinctive hand-like tracks they leave.

hind   front   2¼ in.

Raccoon

Raccoon foraging for food in camp area.

Small Animals

These ubiquitous rodents inhabit the ground, the trees, perhaps even your attic, and represent a fair percentage of local roadkill. Last year's squirrel census alone reported 183 million in the Tahoe basin.

California Ground Squirrel—These squirrels have large bodies like the gray squirrels but have much smaller tails. They have a mottled brown coat and a silver saddle over the shoulder. They spend most of their time on the ground and are very busy all summer getting fattened up to hibernate through the winter.

Chickaree or Douglas Squirrel—This medium-sized dark brown squirrel has a reddish tinge on its back, a white belly, and a bushy tail with a silver tip. Chickarees stay active all winter and make a short explosive *quer-o* sound.

If you hear fir cones crashing down to the ground, and see the mangled remains of the soft cones sitting on a stump, you will know you are in chickaree country. These squirrels love to climb trees and drop the cones for later, when they remove the entire cone, piece by piece, in order to get to the tasty seeds inside.

Golden-mantled Ground Squirrel and Chipmunk—What is the difference between a chipmunk and the golden-mantled ground squirrel? A chipmunk is smaller, and has lines on its back that go all the way over its head. The Tahoe area's most common squirrel, the golden-mantled, has a lovely white band bordered by black running up each side of its back and ending at its shoulders. Both species eat seeds, grasses, and fruit.

Golden-mantled ground squirrel.

17

Western Flying Squirrel—These small brown squirrels (smaller than a chickaree) are very friendly and social, but since they are nocturnal most people will not have the opportunity to see one. They actually glide through the air from tree branch to branch. Like the Western gray squirrel, the flying squirrel remains active all winter.

Western Gray Squirrel—Larger than either the chickaree or ground squirrel, the gray squirrel also lives in the area but in smaller numbers. It has a uniform gray body and a long, broad tail. Like the chickaree, and unlike the ground squirrels and chipmunks, the gray squirrel is active all winter. It loves to sit in trees and "laugh" at cats and dogs, which stare at it with evil intent.

Pika or Cony—The pika is smaller than a chipmunk, light brown in color, and lives primarily in high rocky areas. It looks like a cross between a chipmunk and a small rabbit (and is in the same animal order as the latter) with shorter ears. It makes a peeping noise.

Birds

American Robin—Slightly smaller than the Steller's jay, the robin has a similar physique and is a frequent summer visitor to Lake Tahoe. With its brick-red breast, yellow bill, and gray back, the robin cheerily hops through the understory of local woods or meadows, looking for insects or worms.

Bald Eagle—A very large, majestic black bird with white head, the bald eagle occasionally is spotted flying near water, perched on a large tree, or riding the updrafts. I remember watching an eagle fly along the lakeshore, when suddenly two ospreys began to chase it; the three completed some incredible acrobatic stunts before the ospreys gave up.

Perhaps the eagle had ventured too near the osprey nest. Count yourself lucky if you see one of these rarer raptors.

Blue Grouse—You are more likely to hear a blue grouse than to see one. Males vocalize a very low, bass-drum *brrrmmmmmm, brrrmmmmm, brrrm-mmmm* sound. Females are large, plump birds about the size of a pheasant or chicken. Their plumage is brownish gray with some white feathers near the neck. They can sometimes be seen in trees or brush. Breaking cover, they startle you as they suddenly take flight with a loud *wap, wap, wap* of wings. This bird can commonly be seen or heard in heavily wooded sections on the west shore, including Desolation Wilderness and areas north of Tahoe City.

Grouse.

Canada Goose—Commonly seen along Tahoe beaches and in parks, this large grayish-tan goose has a black head and neck, and a prominent white chin. Though geese are known to steal food from unsuspecting small children, they are beautiful when flying in their A-line formations. Less beautiful are the copious amounts of droppings they leave, making a trip to many a Tahoe beach akin to walking through the room of a teenager (messy but not dangerous).

Clark's Nutcracker—With a shape and sound similar to the Steller's jay, this light gray bird has black wings with white patches. Seen at treeline along high ridgetops, very much Tahoe Rim Trail country, Clark nutcrackers make a loud and slow *flap, flap, flap* with its wings as it flies from tree to tree. It prefers whitebark pines; a single bird can bury thousands of pine seeds in a summer season.

Mountain Chickadee—Perhaps the most common bird in the Tahoe woods, the small chickadee (about 5 inches long) is light gray with a black cap and white line over each eye. Usually quiet, this active bird may be best known for its call, which many people say sounds like *cheese, burrr, gerrrr*; others claim its call sounds more like *tsick-a-dee-dee-dee*. You be the judge. Maybe it just sounds like the voice of a chickadee.

Mountain Quail—California's state bird is small to medium-sized and slightly chunky. You can identify it by the little standard issuing from the top of its head, its gray to brown coloring, and the way it scurries away into nearby brush. It stays close to the ground under bushes near sunny open areas and water sources. Since quail convene in coveys, once you spot one, you will likely hear and see others.

Osprey—Another rare bird, the osprey is best known for its ability to swoop down and catch fish in its talons. The osprey is a little smaller than an eagle, with brown feathers on its back and white feathers on its breast. When flying above you, it appears mostly white, but while sitting in a nest with wings tucked, it can appear mostly brown. The osprey makes a high-pitched squeak and can be seen along the lakeshore or high up in large nests it has built out of sticks at the top of dead trees.

Owl—Various species of owl inhabit the Tahoe area. Primarily nocturnal, they live in the deep woods and are more likely to be heard than seen. While the calls of owls vary with the species, in general you can hear a deep *who, who, who*. Owls have large, round faces with piercing front-facing eyes perfect for late night hunting. Some species have catlike ear tufts that stick straight up.

Steller's Jay—The seemingly ubiquitous Steller's jay is most often found at lake-level elevations and in campgrounds. It is medium-size with a dark blue body and a mantle, throat and crest that are black.

Its aggressive raucous cry or squawk is distinctive. It will eat your potato chips and raid your snack packs, yet many Eastern birders delight in seeing this bird for the first time.

Western Tanager—Though somewhat uncommon, the tanager is one of the most colorful birds in the Tahoe area. The male has a red head, a bright yellow body, and black wings. The female is also bright yellow, but lacks the red head. Try to spot this small- to medium-sized bird (bigger than a chickadee, smaller than a Steller's jay) flitting from tree to tree.

Amphibians and Reptiles

Pacific Tree Frog—These tiny frogs can be heard in many Sierra locales. They are especially common in the grassy area around Twin Lakes, so if you're walking to these lakes be careful not to step on them. About 1 inch long, the frogs are brown or green with black eye stripes. Though called tree frogs, they have no special preference for trees and are just as comfortable on the ground or in the grass.

Snakes—Several snakes live in the Tahoe area. Happily for area hikers, the *rattlesnake* is not common among them. The most common snake in the Tahoe area is the *garter snake*. It is about 2 feet long or less, slender with a tail tapered to a sharp tip. The garter snake has a black or gray upper surface with a yellow line along its back. While for the most part it is harmless, if handled it may discharge a foul-smelling liquid. Less common to this area is the *rubber boa*. A wonder to behold, this docile, harmless small brown snake is usually less than 2 feet long. With its smooth skin, it looks like a worm on steroids.

Western Fence Lizard—This 6 to 9 inch lizard is often found in dry areas lounging on a rock or running to escape your big feet. The scaly skin of the lizard is gray and they are often seen doing little "push-ups" on the rocks, exposing their blue bellies.

Insects

Bees, Yellow Jackets, and Wasps—Honeybees and bumblebees quietly go about their business of pollinating flowers and rarely sting people. Yellow jackets, even though they look like a bee, are actually a form of wasp. After an above-average winter snowfall, especially in a season with a lot of spring moisture and cold temperatures, yellow jackets are found in small numbers. In drought conditions, however, yellow jackets multiply, and by late summer and fall they can be a nuisance. They are ferocious predators and meat-eaters and their stings can be painful and cause swelling. These wasps can nest in the ground or in a trailside log. If you get too close to their nests, they will come out in force to sting you. Wasps are most active from midday to just after sunset.

Mosquitoes—These pesky little critters can be a problem from mid-June through mid-July throughout the Tahoe area. The timing of their emergence from the shadows of spring, however, depends on the quantity of precipitation that arrived during winter and how quickly the snowpack melts. Mosquitoes are active at dusk and dawn and are prevalent in shady forest areas, as well as in and near meadows, along a lakeshore, near creeks and any body of standing water or moist area. They like especially small, shallow bodies of water where they breed. To *avoid* mosquitoes, either pack a lot of insect repellent, take to a granite mountain or ridgetop area, or pray for wind.

Fish

Fish have not been seen recently on the Tahoe Rim Trail, but there are some in the streams and lakes that you might pass. Here are the few to look out for:

Brook Trout—Not a true trout, but a char, its lighter colored spots on a dark green-gray background distinguish the brook. It also has a yellow- to ruddy-colored underbelly. It can be found in any Sierra water source.

Brown Trout—Hugging river bottoms, the brown trout sports an olive green to cinnamon brown coloring with reddish spots along their sides. These fish were imported into the Sierra from Germany and Scotland.

Cutthroat Trout—The most common fish in the mountain lakes and streams, the cutthroat can be identified by its red, orange or yellow "slash" marks under each jaw. It is sometimes called the spotted trout.

Mackinaw or Lake Trout—Incorrectly blamed for eliminating the cutthroat from Lake Tahoe, the Mackinaw trout is also a char family member like the brooky mentioned above. It is the least colorful of all the Sierra fish, gray with some yellow speckles that brighten during spawning season. It grows to a large size; every year 20- to 30-pound mackinaws are caught in Lake Tahoe and Donner Lake, and 10-pound fish are common.

Rainbow Trout—With a bluish-gray to gray-green back, silvery belly, and dark black speckles, the rainbow's most distinctive mark is a red streak down each side. Mountain men and prospectors introduced rainbows into the Sierra in the 1800s.

Kokanee Salmon—Introduced in the 1940s into the Tahoe area lakes, the Kokanee can be found here still. It has a robust body and dusky, olive to bluish coloring. It is silvery on its underside and nests in bottom gravel like the rainbow trout. During their fall spawning run, they turn bright red and can be found in large numbers in Taylor Creek, on Lake Tahoe's South Shore. Sometimes they are also found in smaller numbers spawning up Eagle Creek, right next to the Vikingsholm Castle near Emerald Bay.

Trees

White Fir—Probably the most common tree in the Tahoe Basin, white fir typically grows below 6500' in elevation (although they are sometimes seen up to 7500'). They have gray bark and short, bunched needles that have an average length of 1.5 to 2 inches and a flat appearance. The bark of younger trees is somewhat smooth; as the trees age, the bark gets rougher and more like that of other pine and fir trees. The light green upright cones are soft and found scattered about the woods—the work of chickarees. During the drought of the early 1990s, these firs died in extensive numbers after an insufficient water supply made them vulnerable to disease and beetle infestations.

Red Fir—White firs' red cousin dominates the landscape in some areas above 6500', often living in dense stands. The red fir needle bunches are tighter than those of the white fir, curve inward, and grow to over an inch long. The bark is reddish-brown to gray and the tree sprouts mid-sized cones of 6 to 9 inches as compared to the shorter ones of white fir (3 to 5 inches).

Jeffrey Pine—Jeffrey Pine is the dominant pine tree in much of the Tahoe Sierra and, though it is especially prevalent near lake level, it can grow at elevations up to 8000'. Jeffrey pine can reach a height of 180 feet. It has thick gray to reddish bark, which turns redder as the tree matures, and smells like butterscotch, vanilla or pineapple depending on what kind of nose you have. It also has large roundish cones with up-turning prickles and long needles of three.

Ponderosa or Western Yellow Pine—Similar to the Jeffrey, the ponderosa prefers lower elevations, usually below 6500' and grows in smaller numbers near Lake Tahoe. It has yellowish to reddish-brown bark and often reaches heights of 100 feet. Like Jeffrey pine, ponderosa also has long needles of three. Ponderosa pine cone prickles stick up and out, while the Jeffrey's turn up and in (remember "gentle Jeffrey" or "prickly ponderosa"). In some areas, a hybridized combination of Jeffrey and ponderosa is found, making identification difficult.

Lodgepole Pine—This usually straight tree (hence its value as a lodge pole for Native Americans) is very common in a variety of soil conditions from below 6000' to over 9000' in elevation. It has thin, scaly, light gray and sappy bark, and small cones. The needles are in bunches of two and can be made into an "L" for lodgepole. The tree prefers wet areas and its presence often signals mosquito territory.

Sugar Pine—These beautiful, majestic trees can reach a height of 250 feet. They are uncommon above 6500' and rare in lower elevations since most were cut down for lumber at the end of the 19th century. Sugar pine has long cylindrical cones that grow 10 to 16 inches downward from the tips of long graceful branches. John Muir said of the sugar pine that it "is the noblest pine yet discovered, sur-

Twin Peaks with firs and pines in foreground.

passing all others not merely in size but also in kingly beauty and majesty."

Western White Pine—These trees grow at higher elevations of 7000' to 9000' and can reach 150 feet in height although they are usually much smaller because of the harsh conditions in which they live. Like the whitebark pine, the western white pine has needles that come in clusters of five. Its cone resembles that of the sugar pine though it is shorter (6 to 8 inches) and narrower. The upper branches of a western white pine, also known as silver pine, turn upward at their tips. Mature trees have a distinctive checkerboard pattern on their bark.

Whitebark Pine—This high elevation tree is usually found near mountaintops and is easily mistaken for a lodgepole pine. The tree has short stiff needles clustered in groups of five (while the lodgepole needles are in groups of two). The bark is gray-white, and the cones are small and dark brown. It is also common to see them near the tops of peaks in a shrub-like formation called *krummholz* where they may only stand a foot or so high.

Aspen or Quaking Aspen—The Sierra's most colorful deciduous tree derives its name from the appearance it has when its leaves "quake" in gentle breezes or wind storms. With white bark and oval-shaped leaves, aspens are common in wet and moist areas, along creek beds, near springs, and in meadows. Their presence can indicate a ground-water source. Aspen trees throw out "shooters" of smaller trees, which grow up around the base of their trunks; a single tree may put out dozens of shooters and thus a whole grove may have started with one tree. This tree provides most of the fall yellow and gold color.

Incense Cedar—These trees can grow to a height of 150 feet. Incense cedar is commonly found near the lake (6200') with an upper elevation of around 6500', a little higher in sunny locations. Incense cedars have red to cinnamon-brown flaky bark, and dark green short needles, which lie in flat feathery groupings

Mountain Hemlock—Mountain hemlock prefers high snow areas above 7000' and are common above 8000' in many north-facing areas along the Tahoe Rim Trail, generally in areas of maximum snow pack. A beautiful and majestic tree reaching heights of 25 to 100 feet, with smaller trees at the highest elevations, mountain hemlock has short dark green needles that grow on branches that cover the tree from bottom to top. The branches have a gentle sloping appearance; the cones are small and dark brown. What makes the mountain hemlock especially magical is the way the top of the tree droops over like a wizard's hat.

Western (Sierra) Juniper—Often junipers are found in dry, rocky areas at higher elevations particularly in the Desolation Wilderness. Junipers over 1000 years old have been found in the Tahoe area. They have an appearance similar to incense cedars with reddish, brown bark. They rarely exceed 50 feet in height. Those growing in windy, exposed areas may be twisted and gnarled. The best way to tell the difference between juniper and incense cedar is that juniper has blueberry-like cones, and is usually found at higher elevations.

Wonderful Wildflowers

Wet Areas: Meadows, Stream Banks and Springs

Corn Lily—This poisonous plant looks somewhat like a stalk of corn, but smells like cabbage. Not only is the poison deadly, but it has been reported to turn its victims green. Corn lilies start out like a big cigar roll popping out of the moist meadows in the spring. By late summer it has grown 3 to 6 feet tall. At the top of its broad-leaf stalk, it shows a large grouping of cream-white flowers.

Cow Parsnip—A large wildflower with huge maple-shaped leaves, cow parsnip stalks can reach up to 10 feet tall but average 4 to 5 feet. It is often found in meadows, along creeks, or in other moist areas. It has several tall stalks with tight white button flowers that look like miniature cauliflower heads at the top.

Crimson Columbine—The most commonly seen columbine of the Tahoe area has numerous bright red-orange flowers that look like miniature Chinese lanterns hanging off tall thin stalks. It grows to about 3 feet high in moist meadow areas and along streambeds.

Corn lilies.

Delphinium or Larkspur—Towering larkspur or larkspur delphinium have tall narrow stalks with beautiful small purple flowers that bloom all along the stalks. They are found in large numbers in some meadow and stream areas and provide a dramatic display, especially when they reach their maximum height of 6 to 8 feet. *Nuttall's larkspur* is a smaller variety at only about 1 foot high; it is found in limited numbers in dry or wet areas.

Elephant Heads—Sprouting off the foot-tall green stalks are numerous tiny pink flowers that have little trunks and elephant-shaped ears. While not as showy as other meadow plants like columbine and tiger lilies, elephant heads are often seen in spring and early summer in Tahoe Meadows and especially in Meiss Meadows.

Monkeyflower—There are 11 species of this plant in the Tahoe area, all having flowers supposedly

29

resembling little monkey faces. The most common are the pink Lewis' monkeyflower and the yellow common monkeyflower. They favor the banks of small streams or seeps throughout the Tahoe area.

Monkshood—This relatively uncommon plant is found in moist areas. Its large deep purple flower resembles a monk's cowl. A tall plant that can reach 6 feet, monkshood grows among the tremendous variety of flowers found near Marlette Lake as well as in the Page Meadows area.

Tiger lily.

Shooting Stars—Found in moist meadow areas, shooting stars have delicate petals that bend back to expose the darker stamens, thus making them like streaking night stars. The *alpine shooting star* has pink flowers, while the *Jeffrey's* has a purple-to-pink flower with a black point and a small band of yellow just above the black.

Tiger (Alpine) Lily—Often found with columbine in wet or marshy areas, the tiger lily can grow 4 to 6 feet tall and is a wonderful visual treat with bright orange flowers speckled with brown.

Dry and Sunny Areas

Checkermallow—Along with mule ears, this is perhaps the commonest flower in dry, volcanic areas. It is found at lake level and up to over 9000' and is a low-lying flower with small pinkish-purple cups threaded by white veins.

Douglas or Sierra Wallflower—This bright-yellow flowered plant is common in dry areas and on rocky slopes. A member of the mustard family, it has a big cluster of little yellow petals forming a ball atop a straight green stem. It reaches a height of 1 to 3 feet.

Fireweed—Fireweed grows in profusion along old road cuts and areas that were recently burned, disturbed, or where most of the plant cover has been removed. The plants are 3 to 4 feet high and covered with bright pink flowers.

Horsemint—Horsemint is found in abundance in dry meadows and rocky flats (Tahoe Meadows is one example). It is identifiable by its purple corn-cone group of flowers situated on top of a green stem with many green leaves. It is related to pennyroyal.

Mariposa Lily—The beautiful round white flowers of the Mariposa lily have a purple-to-black center and a delicate appearance. Three cream-white petals form a small bowl. This plant is usually less than 6 inches tall and prefers dry or sandy soil on sunny slopes.

Mountain Pennyroyal or Coyote Mint—This common flower grows in open forests and along volcanic slopes. A member of the mint family, pennyroyal has white or pink flower clusters atop upright stalks. It provides a strong mint smell as you walk by.

(Top)
Fireweed.

(Bottom)
Mariposa lily.

Mule Ears—In areas with open, south-facing slopes, and particularly with volcanic soils, the mule ears

31

are often the dominant flower species. They can cover acres of land with very few other plants in view. When you see a field of mule ears, you will also smell them as they have a strong odor. Big yellow sunflowers and large leaves that resemble the ears of a mule lend the plant its name. In the fall, the leaves dry up and turn brown, and make a rustling noise in the wind.

Prettyface—These relatively common flowers grow close to the ground and have 6 light yellow petals at the end of each flower stem. Each petal has a small dark purple line extending toward its tip. Large groups of "pretty faces" can be found looking at you from dry soil.

Scarlet Gilia—The bright red-orange beauty of scarlet gilia is startling to behold when it appears in the dry sandy forest and on open slopes. It can get up to 3-feet tall and has many bright trumpet-shaped flowers.

Deep Forest Pinedrops—The pinedrop is a saprophyte, which means that the plant obtains its nutrients from decaying vegetation in the ground rather than through photosynthesis. Pinedrops grow to 3-feet tall and have orange-red to reddish-brown stalks with numerous little curly cues coming off the sides of each narrow stalk. After they die they often remain standing for years, turning dark as years go by.

Snowplant.

Snowplant—Snowplants are also saprophytes and do not require sunlight to grow; they appear from under trees or in dense forest areas. They are long and cylindrical (from 6 inches to 1 foot high) and a bright red color. Snowplant shoots straight out of the ground like a huge asparagus stalk, adding a splash of red color to the shade of the forest.

Mixed Wet or Dry Areas

Asters and Daisies—There are several species of these sunflowers that have pale purple petals circling a disk of yellow or gold. The *western aster* and *wandering daisy* are both quite common in the Tahoe area. Both plants grow up to 2 feet tall, although they are usually shorter, and occur up to 9000'. They prefer moist over dry settings.

Aster.

Explorer's Gentian—This late-season bloomer has deep blue or purple tubular-shaped flowers. Light dots speckle the inside of the petals. Found in moist or rocky terrain, gentian provides a bit of bright color when many summertime flowers have come and gone.

Paintbrush—The orange *Red Applegate's paintbrush* and the *giant red paintbrush* are the two species most commonly seen in the Tahoe area. Both have flowers that look like the brush end of a bright orange and red paintbrush. Often they are called Indian paintbrush. These and other species can be found on dry slopes to wet meadows, up to 9000'.

Paintbrush.

Shrubs and Bushes

Buckthorn, Snowbush or Mountain Whitethorn—This plant with many names grows along disturbed areas, along trails, and has lots of narrow white branches with spiny, thorn-like tips; when flattened by the snow, these branches lay down over the trail. I call it "mountain bikers' menace" because its thorns can puncture tires. Whitethorn is about 3 to 4 feet tall and spreads out over 5 to 10 feet. It has small ovate-shaped whitish/green leaves. Often the plants are so thick that it is

33

difficult to determine where one plant ends and another begins.

Chinquapin—This common plant was named after a condominium project north of Tahoe City (or was it the other way around)? Chinquapin is a bushy shrub related to oaks, that inhabits dry slopes and rocky ridges, and frequently grows near manzanita bushes. The narrow leaves of this 2 to 4 foot tall plant are up to 3 inches long, yellow-green on the top, and yellow-brown underneath. Chinquapin produces yellow-green, spring seedpods.

Huckleberry Oak—One of the most common plants in this area, huckleberry oak typically gets to about 3 feet high and grows on dry-south facing slopes. It has small leathery ovate leaves of medium to dark green. At the end of the narrow stalks you may see a light green acorn.

Manzanita—While there are five species of manzanita in the Sierra, only two are commonly seen in the Tahoe area. *Greenleaf manzanita* is widespread in dryer areas over a wide elevation range. Its smooth bark is dark red or reddish-brown with shiny, bright green leaves and it grows to about 3 to 5 feet tall. Manzanita has lots of rigid, crooked thick branches. In the spring they put out tiny pink flowers that supposedly look like little apples ("manzanita" is Spanish for little apple). *Pinemat manzanita*, with similar leaves and stalks, is a smaller plant that grows to about a foot tall; it likes to form a carpet along the ground or over the top of granite rocks. Pinemat manzanita usually grows at a higher altitude than its greenleaf cousin.

Red Mountain Heather—This dwarfish bush has dark green conifer-like needles and clusters of small bright pink or red flowers on the top of short stalks. It grows at high elevations throughout the Tahoe area, along some lakeshores, and in the Desolation

Wilderness. This fragile plant is a thick ground cover running alongside the trail so take care not to step on it.

Squaw Carpet or Mahala Mat—Thick patches as much as 10 to 20 feet across are made up of holly-like leaves carpeting the ground. In the spring, clusters of small blue-to-violet flowers grow among the sharp-edged leaves.

Thimbleberry—They may not keep you from starving in the woods, but thimbleberries are edible and quite tasty when they ripen in late August and September. They are in the same family as blackberries and raspberries and you will not be surprised to hear that the berries look like little thimbles. This bush is usually found in large groups lying close along the ground near streams and in other shady moist areas. Thimbleberry has large leaves that resemble a maple leaf with three to five pointed lobes. The showy white flowers bloom in early summer.

Tobacco Brush—Some say the strong pungent aroma of tobacco brush is sensuous and aromatic; to me, it smells like tobacco. With large, shiny, dark greenish-blue leaves, the plant grows up to 5 feet tall and has numerous small white flowers. Tobacco brush likes dry disturbed areas along road cuts and trails and can become the locally dominant plant.

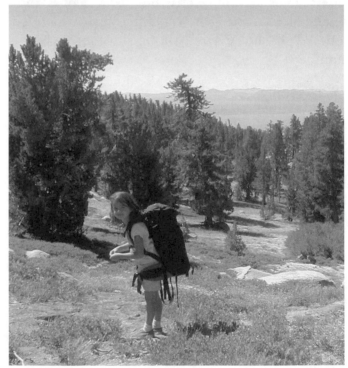

(Top)
Trailblazers'
handiwork near
Mt. Baldy.

(Bottom)
Which is bigger
. . . Hannah or
the backpack?

CHAPTER 3

Let's All Get Along: A Trail for Everyone

The goal of the Tahoe Rim Trail Association is for all users to safely use and enjoy the trail while working to maintain and protect it. It is important that all trail users pleasantly coexist. This comes down to understanding and being courteous to one another, and through recognizing that we are all out there to have fun. Hikers make less of an impact on the Tahoe Rim Trail than mountain bikers. Although horse traffic has the greatest impact on the quality of the trail, there are far fewer horseback riders than other trail users. The only way to make sure that relations between the user groups improve, and that the TRT is maintained, is for users to follow some simple rules.

Rules for Mountain Bikers

When the Tahoe Rim Trail was first constructed, hiking and horseback riding were allowed, but mountain biking was prohibited on the entire trail. As opposition to mountain bike use declined and the numbers of riders increased, much more of the trail has been opened to bikers. Where bikes *are* allowed, bike riders are often the major trail users. Now you can ride a mountain bike on over half the trail.

While people both hike and ride, there can still be tension between the different types of trail users. Since mountain bikers have become major trail users and bike use continues to be controversial in some eyes, mountain bikers should make an extra effort to be courteous and sensitive to the environment by remaining on the maintained trails. They should urge friends and others that they meet to do so as well.

Cycling is a legitimate use of backcountry trails, but there are responsibilities that all bikers are expected to assume. Hikers have complained about encountering bikers on sections of the trail closed to biking, while many hikers, trail runners, or horseback riders have been surprised or threatened by bikers speeding past.

The Tahoe Rim Trail Association has published the following rules of the trail for bikers, which are called Dirt Users' Hints (see sidebar).

Mountain bikers on the trail between Tahoe Meadows and Tunnel Creek.

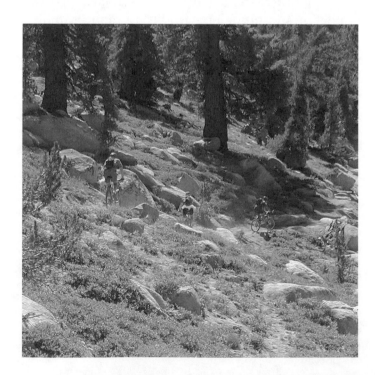

Dirt Users' Hints (DUH)

Preserve the Dirt

🚲 *Skidding destroys trails.* Learn to use both brakes like the pros.

🚲 *Stay on the trail!* Deadfall trees? Snowbanks? Hurdle them, you're tough.

🚲 *Stay in the center of the trail.* Preserve a single-track trail as a single track.

🚲 *Yes, you do need written, land-agency approval to build your dream trail.*

🚲 *Join multi-use maintenance crews.* Help preserve the trail's integrity.

Respect Other Users

🚲 *Pass others at a socially acceptable velocity*—for them!

🚲 *Ring a bell, smile, and say hello.*

🚲 *Horses think you want to eat them.* Act accordingly; wait on the lower side of the trail.

🚲 *Wear a helmet*, or others will have to drag your corpse back to your loved ones.

🚲 *Ride only open trails.* Remember the PCT, wilderness areas, and several other portions of the Tahoe Rim Trail are closed to bikes. You need to know if the portion of trail you are on is permissible for bikes.

🚲 *Leave nothing of your presence behind.* That includes trash, skid trenches, and off-trail tracks.

Sharing the Trail with Horses

While horseback riding can cause more damage to trails than any other use, equestrians account for a smaller percentage of trail users. Many equestrians, too, are actively involved in trail maintenance and construction. In my experience, horseback riders are courteous and willing to work with other users to share the trails.

Depending on individual circumstances, and as a practical matter, all users should yield to each other. In general, hikers should yield to horses, while mountain bikers must yield to both hikers and horses: in other words, horses have the right-of-way on the trail. In the mid-1990s an article appeared in the Tahoe Rim Trail *Newsletter* written by Sonja Willits, a woman with years of experience riding horses on Sierra trails. Willits did a good job of explaining trail use from the horse's point of view. With her permission, I've summarized the main points below.

- *A horse believes that everything will eat it until proven otherwise.* The first instinct of many horses is to run away, which can endanger both horse and rider, as well as anyone in the flight path who could get trampled or knocked off the trail. It is the job of all humans—equestrians, hikers, and mountain bikers—to assure the horse that no harm is intended.

- *When you are approaching a horse from behind, be sure to talk to the rider.* This lets the horse know that you are not something that will hurt it. A bike that comes speeding up from behind a horse can severely frighten it. Be particularly cautious when rounding blind corners—horse riders often can't hear you coming.

- *When you see a horse coming toward you on the trail, talk to the rider.* Again, this soothes the horse and assures it that you are not a threat.

- *When approaching a horse going down a hill, pull over to the downhill slope of the trail and allow the horse to pass.* Spooked horses often want to go uphill.

- *If you are in a group of more than one biker or hiker, encourage everyone to move to the same side of the trail when you encounter horses.* Horses can feel trapped between you if you are standing on either side of the trail. An entrapped horse is not a good thing.

🐎 *Wait to change clothes, repack your backpack, or make any sudden moves until the horses have passed.* While you are stopped, waiting for a horse to go by, it may seem perfectly fine to take off a shirt or rearrange things. As far as the horse is concerned, your movement and changed appearance may add to its feelings of being threatened.

Most horseback riders will move off the trail when it is easy for them to do so. They don't expect hikers and bike riders to give way all the time, particularly when the trail is especially narrow or precarious. However, it is the job of bike riders and hikers to step to the side first, and it is important to have some basic understanding of horse and rider psychology in order to be a conscientious sharer of the trail.

Hikers Take Note

In recent years, mountain bikers have taken great strides toward more environmentally and socially-sensitive use of the trails. It is also the responsibility of hikers to make an extra effort to get along with other trail users. If hikers use common sense and follow the basic rules of courtesy, everyone will benefit and more fully enjoy the trail. If hikers don't reciprocate, they may turn into the dreaded "Inconsiderate Backcountry Blockhead" (see sidebar). Don't let this happen to you!

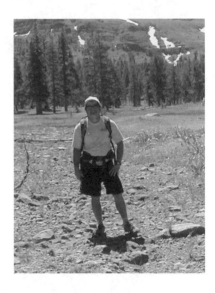

Author—not an inconsiderate blockhead —in the Meiss Meadows area.

*How To Be an
Inconsiderate
Backcountry
Blockhead.*

Tim's Quick Tips for How To Be an Inconsiderate Backcountry Blockhead

✕ Make a lot of noise.

✕ While people are relaxing and enjoying the quiet at a mountain lake, yell at your friends on the other side of the lake.

✕ Let your dogs bark; when they take a swim, let them shake off on people you don't know.

✕ While you are walking along on the trail, talk loudly so that everyone within a half mile can hear you.

✕ If you are camping, make lots of noise late at night and again early in the morning. When you are in the quiet woods, it's party time!

✕ Loud stereos especially appeal to your average nature lover.

✕ Camp or sit close to other people. When you encounter a solitary person at a beautiful mountain lake, they obviously need some companionship and nonstop chatter.

✕ Don't worry about your garbage; someone else will pick it up. Anyway, it should biodegrade in a couple thousand years. Leave things in your campsite, so everyone knows you were there. It's a way to mark the good spots.

✕ Stay on the trail in people's way when they are trying to get by. If people are riding up a hill, stand in their way so they have to get off their bikes; they will enjoy the struggle to get back in their pedals on a steep hill.

✕ When you are walking or riding along the trail, ignore someone else wanting to pass. What's the hurry?

✕ Wash your dishes and clean your fish in streams and lakes. Fish thrive on detergent and consider bits of processed cheese to be great delicacies.

✕ Feed the animals. That way you help train them to get food from the next hiker who comes along. Backpackers get to practice the art of keeping animals out of their packs in the middle of the night. You can train some chipmunks and squirrels so well that they will practically jump into your lap to get a snack. While they can carry bubonic plague, the risk is a small price for well-trained squirrels.

✕ Leaving food out at night for bears is even more fun. The sound of a bear rampaging through your camp gives you a better rush than a double espresso.

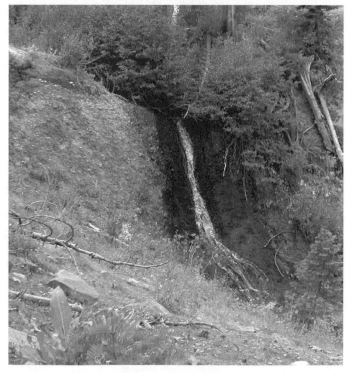

*(Top)
Emerald Bay.
Fanette Island
is in the
foreground,
Mt. Tallac and
Maggies Peaks
are in the
background.*

*(Bottom)
McCloud Falls
in Ward
Canyon.*

CHAPTER 4

Weather, Water, and When to Go

Some basic knowledge about the weather and water availability in the Lake Tahoe area and along its Rim Trail will help you plan a safe and enjoyable trip. All outdoor recreational activities in the Sierra are greatly affected by weather conditions. Of particular relevance is how much precipitation, usually in the form of snow, occurred the previous winter. Sierra Nevada "winters" come in a wide variety of sizes and time frames. In some years, it begins to snow in October and doesn't stop until June. After a year like that, hiking on dry land is out of the question until the middle of July in most areas. The following winter may not see snow until late January, and then make up for it by dropping a lot of snow through May (a great year for late fall hiking). One season might have early heavy snow, followed by light snow, and then warm temperatures after February: this bodes well for those who want to get into the woods early to enjoy great wildflower displays and decent water availability.

Snow Pack

The areas of highest elevation around Lake Tahoe often receive over 600 inches of snow annually. There are several factors for determining whether the place you want to go will be out of the snow in the spring or summer and some general rules governing the area's snow pack. Winter storms arrive primarily from the west, leaving lots of snow near the Sierra crest. There is less snow as you travel farther east from the mountaintops. The west side of Lake Tahoe gets considerably more snow than the east. (The east shore gets about 30 percent less snow on average at the same elevations as the west shore.)

Elevation—The amount of snow is greatly determined by elevation. As cold air lifts and passes over higher terrain, the likelihood and amount of precipitation increase. Storms progress across land forms and temperatures drop as you go up in elevation; the higher you go, the more likely it is that the precipitation will be snow. Over the course of a season, high elevations receive considerably more snow than lower elevations.

Which Way the Mountain Faces—Snow melts at different rates depending on which direction the mountain is facing and which side of the mountain you are on: north-facing slopes get less sun and stay cooler. Here, the snow melts more slowly. The difference between the snow pack on a north or south-facing slope can be quite surprising; it is not unusual to see five feet of snow on a north-facing slope, while on the south-facing slope the ground is bare and wildflowers are coming up.

Although the difference between north and south is more pronounced, east-facing slopes are also cooler and will have more snow than west-facing slopes. A classic example in the Tahoe area of the north–south difference is Emerald Bay. The Vickingsholm Trail and the trail along Emerald Bay to Emerald Point on the south-facing side of the bay, are free of snow in most years at least one

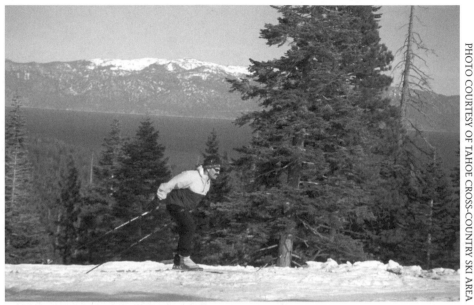

month before the trails on the north-facing side of the bay.

Lee of the Mountains: Away from the Wind and the Rain—The farther east you travel away from the western face of the mountains, the less likely for snow to fall. The mountains block and capture the snow and rain, leaving little moisture for the areas to the east. Consequently, the area around Serene Lakes on Donner Summit gets more snow than *almost* anywhere else in the United States, while just 40 miles to the east, and behind several mountains, Reno frequently receives less precipitation than any other major city in the United States.

The Wind, It Doth Blow—Winter winds create huge snowdrifts that resemble desert sand dunes. What does this mean to a hiker? There are areas where these winter dunes take longer to melt than other snow-packed areas, most commonly on the lee side of ridgetops where cornices form. These cornices can last well into the summer, while all around them wildflowers grow.

47

Trail Use Tip

Early in the season, your best bet for a hike or ride is close to the lake or in the Truckee area (lower elevations and in the lee of the mountains), on the east side of the lake (Carson Range), and at lower elevations. As the season progresses, different areas become available for snow-free travel, moving from east to west, and south-facing to north-facing.

Winter Wonderland

The winter landscape of the Sierra Nevada Mountains is both serene and pristine, with a beauty that you rarely find in the summer. In the winter, a soft white blanket covers the world with cold sparkles reflecting the blue sky. Walking or skiing through new fallen snow, you will find the rarest of gifts—peace and true quiet. In addition to the heavy snow fall in winter, you will also have some sunny winter days that provide wonderful opportunities to get out and enjoy all that deep white powder. Although many people prefer the winter as the time to enjoy the mountains and woods, this can be a more challenging and dangerous time. Unpredictable weather, unsigned trails, and other snow-related hazards are among the risk factors with which you should become familiar. Observe the weather and snow conditions. If the weather is getting bad, be smart, turn around and get out. Continually check your surroundings, observe familiar peaks, creeks, and other landmarks that will allow you to get back to your starting point if you are in a blizzard. Some of the most powerful blizzards can quickly become life-threatening. If you learn about mountain winter conditions and take a few simple precautions, much of the trail and areas in the Lake Tahoe area are great for winter snowshoeing or cross-country skiing.

Land without Visible Trails—The fact that the Tahoe Rim Trail is not signed for winter creates challenges for even the most experienced. Many popular winter spots may have tracks from the people who were there before you, but there are no real trails. You must follow landforms and head for saddles, mountaintops, or flats. Often, you may be heading in a general direction instead of to an exact spot. Know where you are and where you have been, and don't hesitate to follow your own tracks back out to where you began. It becomes even more important to have a map and follow it. Learn how to use a compass.

Dehydration—This is another serious risk when you are hiking, snowshoeing, snowboarding or cross-country skiing. With all that snow around, you still need to drink plenty of water. When the weather is colder, people tend to drink less even though they may actually need as much water as on a hot day. While you are at it, eat. You'll need the energy.

Hypothermia and Frostbite—When the body's core temperature is seriously reduced as a result of exposure to cold and moisture, hypothermia can result. This is a serious condition, aggravated by cold wind and sudden climate changes. The symptoms of hypothermia include shivering, loss of coordination and the ability to do simple tasks, and disorientation and confusion. The treatment is based on common sense: first, get the victim out of the wind and elements. Prevent heat loss by getting the victim into warm, dry clothes (you should be carrying extra clothing in your pack). Get the victim into a sleeping bag, if you have one, and climb in to add your body heat (although, be careful as this may lower your own body temperature). Give the victim warm liquids and high carbohydrate foods.

49

Frostbite is the freezing of body tissues due to prolonged exposure to cold. The most susceptible areas to frostbite are the feet, hands, ears and face. Prevention is the key for both hypothermia and frostbite. Remember a few simple rules: eat high-energy foods and drink plenty of liquids. Keep rested. Wear the right clothing and bring along layers. Don't do something that will get you wet, and get out of the woods if you do get wet on a cold and windy day. Have an extra set of clothes in case you get wet.

Avalanches—Understanding how avalanches occur and how to avoid them is too big a topic for this book, but a few words of warning can help you avoid a tragedy. Remember that you are most vulnerable to avalanche when you are on moderately steep slopes (very steep slopes may not hold enough snow to avalanche), the lee side of mountains, or in gullies. Unstable snow conditions most often occur during or right after a storm; the bigger the storm, the bigger the risk. Obtain an updated avalanche danger report by calling the Truckee Ranger District's hotline at (530) 587-2158. If you plan to do a lot of backcountry travel, you might find two books particularly useful: *The Avalanche Handbook* by Ronald Perla and *The Avalanche Book* by Betsy Armstrong.

Sunburn!—The bright sun makes the snow even more beautiful and white. At the end of the day you have beautiful memories, and one heck of a case of sunburn. Snow reflects the sun's rays like water and can burn your skin quickly. Use sunscreen and wear sunglasses to protect your eyes.

Packing and Dressing for Winter Weather

Aside from sunblock, be sure to carry a basic survival kit! Your kit should include the following items:

✓ Two large plastic leaf bags (to be used as a poncho or emergency shelter in bad weather)

✓ Waterproof matches

✓ A plastic whistle (three short blasts means help)

✓ Candle

✓ Metal cup for melting snow

✓ Duct tape (for repairs, can be wrapped around the top of a ski pole)

✓ Cocoa or other powdered mix

✓ A couple of quarters for emergency phone calls (just in case you can reach a phone).

You have three goals when it comes to clothing yourself for outdoor winter adventures: keep dry, keep warm, and keep cool. To accomplish these goals, wear or pack clothing made of synthetic fibers. They are lightweight and whisk moisture away from your body which will help to keep you warm. Bring several lightweight layers of clothes, including a waterproof outer shell; it will help you stay dry but will allow you to remain cool if the temperature turns warm. Wear a sturdy pair of waterproof boots with two pairs of socks, a thin inner layer of socks made of synthetic fiber and a thicker outer layer of wool or synthetic fiber. Wear water-resistant pants, such as those designed for cross-country skiing; over these, wear a waterproof shell if you are snowshoeing or traveling through deep snow. A hat is essential, whether it is a baseball cap on a warm day or a warm fleece hat on a cold day. And, don't forget gloves: the style depends on the conditions and activity you are doing. If it is warm and you are doing strenuous cross-country skiing, lightweight ski gloves are fine. If you are out hiking or snowshoeing on a cold snowy day, bring a thicker, warmer pair of gloves.

For more information on the best clothing to wear, contact one of the many cross-country ski outfitters and outdoor clothing retailers in the Tahoe area, such as Alpenglow and The Back Country in Tahoe City; Paco's and Sierra Mountaineer in Truckee; Tahoe Sports Ltd. or Cutting Edge Sports in South Lake Tahoe; or REI in Reno, Sacramento or the Bay Area.

Tim's Quick Tips: Avoiding Winter Weather Risks

❆ *Keep an eye on the weather forecasts until right before you leave.* Many great weather sources exist, including local radio and television stations (KCRA-Sacramento, and KOLO-Reno are two of them); The Weather Channel (on cable television); and, these websites— www.weather.com and www.TimsTahoeAdventures.com—are also useful.

❆ *Before setting out, let someone know where you are going and when you plan to return.*

❆ *Bring extra layers of clothing.* The weather may change for the worse even if the forecast is for nice weather.

❆ *Do not venture out unless you know how to navigate without a visible trail.*

❆ *Use a compass and map.*

❆ *Bring your surival kit!*

❆ *Drink lots of water.*

❆ *Avoid situations that cause hypothermia and frostbite.*

Water

Much of the Tahoe Rim Trail is located along ridgetops, a perfect situation for enjoying the sublime views of Lake Tahoe and the surrounding mountains. However, its rim-top location results in a shortage of water along many sections of the trail, especially on the sections along the east shore. Plan ahead and make sure you have enough water to get you through the section you will be hiking. On hot summer days, you will need at least two to three quarts of water.

Be sure to avoid drinking any untreated water in the Sierra Nevada. *Giardia,* a microorganism that occurs in many bodies of water here, can create havoc in your intestines. To prevent *giardia* or other bugs from getting into your system, be sure to filter, boil, or treat with iodine any water that you draw from a natural source.

In each section of the trail described in chapter 6, additional specific water information is provided.

When (and Where) To Go

Winter to Spring

For those who love the snow and winter sports, there are a number of places that are especially attractive and challenging for winter activities. Here are a few of the best spots:

Page Meadows—The easiest way to access Page Meadows in winter is through the Talmont Estates subdivision. From Tahoe City, go 2 miles south on Highway 89 to Pine Avenue. Turn right, then right again on Tahoe Park Heights. Go to the top of the hill where you will take Big Pine, the middle of three road choices. Follow Big Pine to Silvertip and turn left. There is limited parking available at the end of Silvertip. From the end of the road, head west a few hundred yards to the first of several meadows. The area around Page Meadows is especially popular for cross-country skiing and snowshoeing. The terrain is mostly level, perfect for beginners. The meadows are beautiful on a sunny day or at night when the moon is full.

Tahoe Meadows—Located on the south side of Highway 431, the meadow is great for a beginner

53

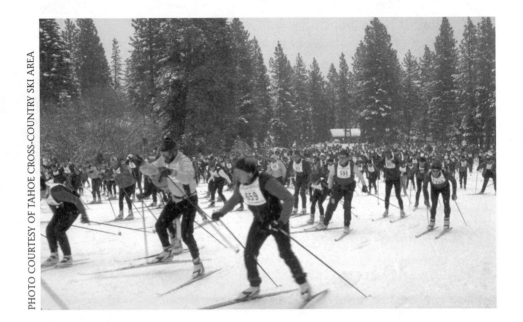

PHOTO COURTESY OF TAHOE CROSS-COUNTRY SKI AREA

on either skis or snowshoes. From Incline Village, drive 7 miles up Highway 431, the Mount Rose Highway. Here, you will see a large treeless area on your right. Park along the road. Both the large open meadow and its surrounding forest are popular for winter sports; in fact, on a weekend you might find this area too crowded. Head south up through the trees to a saddle for extraordinary lake views. You could well be dazzled by lodgepole and whitebark pines covered with hoarfrost.

On the north side of the highway at Tahoe Meadows, the TRT climbs toward the radio tower and Mount Rose, another excellent area to ski or snowshoe. While this route can get quite steep and difficult near the top, the views of Mount Rose and Lake Tahoe from the radio tower are inspiring.

Spooner Lake Cross-Country Ski Area—Located at Spooner Lake near the intersection of Highways 50 and 28, this well-managed cross-country ski area provides access to Marlette Lake, Snow Valley Peak, and the Hobart Road area via over 90 km of beautifully groomed trails, some of which crisscross the Tahoe Rim Trail. Views of Lake Tahoe and the beautiful Snow Valley are seen from the trails. At Spooner Lake Cross-Country, you can rent a rustic log hut during winter or summer. For more information, contact them at (775) 749-5349.

Tahoe Cross-Country Ski Area—Located on Dollar Hill about 2 miles east of Tahoe City along Highway 28, Tahoe Cross Country is the venue for The Great Ski Race from Tahoe City to Truckee (which crosses the Tahoe Rim Trail). This wonderful area provides 65 km of trails through the forests between Mount Watson and Tahoe City. Many of this Nordic center's trails are popular with mountain bikers and hikers in the summer. Contact Tahoe Cross Country at (530) 583-5475.

Kirkwood Cross-Country Ski Area—Kirkwood is located 30 miles south of South Lake Tahoe on Highway 88. It has a network of 80 km of trails with spectacular views of the Carson Pass–Kirkwood area. The Echo to Kirkwood Ski Race, terminating at the Nordic center here, is a popular but difficult race that follows a section of the Tahoe Rim Trail. For more information, call (209) 258-7248.

For additional information on winter trail use, take a look at *Snowshoe Trails of Tahoe* by Michael White, another Wilderness Press author. The Tahoe Nordic Search and Rescue Team also has all kinds of valuable information and they are the guys and gals you will be really happy to see if you get lost in the snow. Some of the information in this section comes from: Tahoe Nordic Search and Rescue Team's Winter Awareness brochure, "A guide to winter preparedness and survival." To obtain a copy, or for more information call (530) 581-4038. Above all else, if you have a phone, IN AN EMERGENCY, CALL 911.

Meadow at the edge of Lake Aloha.

Summer to Fall

Summer and early fall at Tahoe are mostly sunny, warm, and glorious. Nevertheless, afternoon thunderstorms do come up. During some summers there may be no thunderstorms while in other years, they may occur almost daily. Usually storms are scattered, developing—sometimes out of a clear blue sky—during mid-to-late afternoons when the temperatures are warm and a great deal of tropical moisture has moved in from the south. Keep your eye on the large and high darkening clouds moving rather quickly in your general direction. Better yet, check out the weather information channel or local weather broadcasts and plan accordingly. You can also log on to www.theweatherchannel.com or www.TimsTahoeAdventures.com.

The chance of a thunderstorm need not thwart or curtail your plans, but do bring your rain gear.

Sometimes the storm moves swiftly through a specific area and drops only a little rain before it passes. However, if the storm gets exciting and lightning starts to flash, get out as quickly as possible, especially if you are on an exposed peak, near bodies of water, or under tall trees. Avoid areas of high exposure, such as the top of a pass. Dicks Pass, for example, is not a good place to be in a thunderstorm. Avoid the urge to take shelter under a solitary tree in open lands. If you cannot get out of the woods in time, it is best to stay in the forest in an area of similar-sized trees. While lightning can be scary and dangerous, it is also important to remember that it is rare that someone is actually struck by a lightning bolt. Absent a bit of very bad luck, if you take reasonable precautions you should be fine.

Hikers cool their feet.

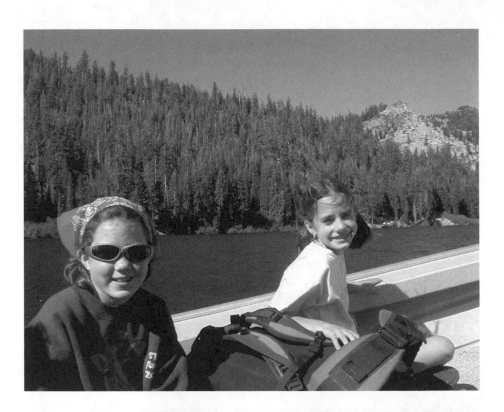

(Top)
Girls love the
Echo Lakes
water taxi.

(Bottom)
Mountain biker
near Armstrong
Pass.

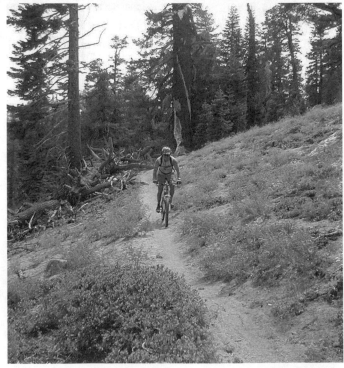

CHAPTER 5

Fun for All and All for Fun: A User's Guide to the Tahoe Rim Trail

During spring, summer, and fall, many types of users enjoy the Tahoe Rim Trail, each with particular needs, all with the same general goal of having fun, enjoying nature, and challenging themselves on the trail. Because one user's mode of transport on the trail—whether it is a pair of legs, a pair of wheels, or four strong horse hooves—can impact another's, this chapter will focus on the different types of users and offer tips and suggestions for a mutually safe and pleasant journey.

A Hiking Paradise

Most people who buy this book probably enjoy hiking already and know the basics: carry plenty of water, wear comfortable boots or shoes, take a map, guidebook and sunscreen, and bring extra clothes in case of a change in the weather. Chapter 6 has complete descriptions of each section of the Tahoe Rim Trail, plus information about short spur trails that hikers can add to customize their

Star Lake.

outings. Every section of the trail offers something unique, whether it is the scenery or the specific challenge of the route.

To get the most out of your journey, take care of a few simple things before you leave. Most importantly, tell someone where you are going, when you expect to be back, and check in when you return. Although the Tahoe Rim Trail is not as isolated as a lot of backcountry areas, you may still be alone on many parts of it. It is only common sense to leave information with a friend or family member as to your general whereabouts. In "Tim's Top Tips For Backcountry Hikers," you will find a checklist of key things to remember when you are planning your Tahoe Rim Trail trek.

Tim's Top Tips For Backcountry Hikers

🐾 Bring more water than you think you will need.

🐾 Don't drink the water in lakes and streams unless you boil, filter, or treat it.

🐾 Carry a First Aid kit. If you take something out, don't forget to restock.

🐾 Dress in layers. Don't wear cotton except on hot dry days in mid-summer.

🐾 Wear good hiking boots or a comfortable athletic shoe. Some hikers prefer the newer high-quality hiking sandals.

🐾 Wear a liner sock and a heavier outer sock.

🐾 Bring enough clothes; temperatures can change quickly.

🐾 Carry and use sunscreen.

🐾 Bring rain gear—the weather can change rapidly in the Sierra.

🐾 Start out early when it is still cool and there are fewer people on the trail.

🐾 Bring a map and this guidebook. A good field guide is also useful to have along.

🐾 Tell someone where you're going and when you expect to return; check in when you return.

🐾 If your knees hurt when you hike, try using a walking stick or two; this tool can make a significant difference when you hike downhill and help to balance you when you are needing to scramble over a rocky section of trail.

🐾 If you have recently come from a much lower altitude, take time to acclimate yourself to a higher altitude before you set off.

Backpacking and Camping

Why not hike the whole Tahoe Rim Trail? Depending on how strong a hiker you are, it takes anywhere from 10 days to 3 weeks to totally encircle Lake Tahoe on this route. Two weeks would be a comfortable period (although two weeks of backpacking and comfort are not usually seen in the same sentence). The TRT is a loop trail so you

61

could start anywhere and end right back where you began.

A backpacking trip of this length requires some major logistical planning. Your primary concerns will be where to camp and where to get water and additional food. Camping is allowed everywhere on the Tahoe Rim Trail except in Desolation Wilderness where you must obtain a permit in order to camp. For more information, call (530) 573-2674. Although permits are not required in Lake Tahoe Nevada State Park, camping is limited here to two primitive campgrounds, each with a pit toilet and picnic tables. For more information, call (775) 831-0494.

To find out where else you can camp, refer to the trail descriptions in Chapter 6. For water availability, review the "Heads Up" section at the beginning of each trail description. If you are hiking in late summer or fall, keep in mind that some of the water spots may have dried up. If you come to a major water source in the fall, be sure to fill up, but be sure to boil, filter, or treat the water before drinking it.

The good news (or bad depending on your perspective) is that a lot of people live at Lake Tahoe who have built communities with stores that carry every amenity you could possibly need.

Road Crossings and Drop-Off Points

Your backpacking trip can be designed so that you can pick up food and supplies at various locations and trailheads along the way. In between the stops, where you may have arranged to meet friends, you will need water. Here is a summary of the road crossings and communities that you will encounter along the TRT.

Desolation Wilderness from near Monument Pass.

Tahoe City (Sections 1 and 8)—The trail route goes right through Tahoe City, a good midway stop-off point if you started your trip at Echo Summit or Kingsbury Grade. As you cross the road from one section of the trail to the next, you will be within 100 yards of a supermarket, and within half a mile of several motels; these are often booked-up in the summer so call ahead and warn them to have the showers ready. Tahoe City is loaded with outfitters who will be happy to sell you any equipment you may have forgotten or need to replace. Check out The Back Country or Alpenglow located near the trail on North Lake Blvd., the main road that goes through the center of town.

Kings Beach (Sections 1 and 2)—The trail crosses Highway 267 at 2.75 miles northwest of Kings Beach. A supermarket is located near the intersection of Highway 267 and Highway 28, with most of the supplies you may need. This road crossing is a good place for a friend to drop off food or water, or you could leave a stash of water here in advance.

63

Very little water is available on the section of trail between Tahoe City and Brockway Summit; when you cross Highway 267, the next water source is a spring beyond Mud Lake, which is over 10 miles away. This spring may run dry by fall, so don't count on it for your only supply.

Incline Village (Sections 2 and 3)—The TRT crosses Highway 431 at 7.7 miles above Incline Village. This is another place to meet your wonderful friends who have brought you fresh supplies. Be sure to load up on water at Ophir Creek, less than a mile along the trail after you cross Highway 431. If you are heading south during a dry year, the next water source directly on the TRT may be over 35 miles away.

Spooner Summit/Highway 50 (Sections 3 and 4)—There are no towns nearby, but this first road crossing in 23 miles may be a good place to stop and get replenished by those now great friends of yours (your "trail angels").

Daggett Pass (Sections 4 and 5)—At the top of Kingsbury Grade, you will have the joy of walking several miles to the next trailhead through a subdivision and the Heavenly Ski Resort. Ah, but they have food and drink and lodging available, and you walk right by the Tramway Market. Perhaps they would even be willing to hold a box for you, so call (775) 588-8666. This may make a good spot for a major stop or planned meeting place. In addition, Stateline and South Lake Tahoe are only 4 miles away down the Kingsbury Grade.

Highway 89, Big Meadow Trailhead (Sections 5 and 6)—You have just hiked 23 grueling miles and you get to the road, and there is nothing except a bathroom. Use it. This is another good drop-off point where your loyal friends can bring you food acquired in nearby South Lake Tahoe or Meyers. If your friends don't show up, or you are in an emergency, Meyers is about 5.3 miles downhill from the trailhead.

Echo Summit/Resort (Sections 6 and 7)—After 17.5 more miles past Big Meadow Trailhead, you reach the Echo Lakes Chalet (530) 659-7207 which has a store. Stock up because Barker Pass Road is 33 miles north. On that road it is an additional 11 miles to the next store. The Echo Chalet has a seasonal post office open during the summer months where you can pick up a package of food that you were smart enough to mail to yourself before you left on your excursion. Or, you can mail food to the next town post office, Tahoe City, 49 miles away.

Barker Pass (Sections 7 and 8)—This remote road crossing is located over 11 miles from Tahoe City via Barker Pass Road and Highway 89, and could work in a pinch as a drop-off point.

Ward Creek Road (Section 8)—The trail crosses this road halfway between Barker Pass and Tahoe City. If necessary, you could have asked someone to meet you at this road crossing to supply moral support and give you the news of the day, but Tahoe City is only five more miles away.

What To Bring in Your Backpack

A few years ago, my good friend and hiking buddy Shannon Raborn hiked the entire 2100 miles of the Appalachian Trail that runs between Georgia and Maine. When she told me what to bring on a spring/summer/fall backpacking trip in the Sierra, I listened. I thank Shannon for her helpful contributions to the following list, which we wrote together.

First, you will want to organize your pack by the object's use. Remember, the less weight and space taken up, the better off you will be as you carry it down (and up and down again) the trail:

Clothes—Hiking shorts, shirts (made of light-weight, preferably light synthetic fibers), warm fleece shirt, rain shell, several pairs of socks, Tevas or water socks (for around camp), baseball hat, warm pants, fleece hat, and gloves.

Toiletries—Toothbrush, toothpaste, vitamins and medications, comb, sunscreen, toilet paper, biode-gradable all purpose soap and scrubby sponge for cleaning pots, pans and your hands. Try to pack any scented product in a scent-proof container and remember to store it in a bear canister when you go to sleep at night.

Camping Supplies—First-aid kit, tent, stuff sack, rope, Thermarest pad, Thermarest chair (a luxury but very nice if you are camping for a long period of time), sleeping bag (lightweight is best), back-packing pillow (another luxury, but it feels SOOOO good!), stove (test it at home to make sure it works if you like to eat cooked food), gas for stove, water fil-ter and/or iodine tablets, water bottles, Camelback (optional but very nice, especially because it en-ables you to carry large amounts of water, nec-essary on the dryer sections of the TRT), trowel (pooper scooper), lighter and/or matches, pot/pan kit, bowl, cup, utensils (spoon, fork, knife), Swiss Army type all-purpose knife, compass, headlamp or flashlight, map, field guides, this book of course, and camera.

If you are "camping light," and the weather forecast does not include rain, *and* it is past mos-quito season (late summer), you could forego the tent and tent fly. If you do not mind going without cooked food, you can also eliminate the stove, stove fuel, and pots and pans. Keeping your clothes to a minimum is another technique to lower weight, but be sure to not cut out something you may need.

Bear Canisters—In areas with lots of bears, bear canisters are essential. Canisters not only work well at keeping out small animals such as squirrels and marmots, but they can serve as a chair or as a wash tub for doing your laundry.

Food—Plan what you need, but keep it light. Remember that John Muir only took some biscuits with him! Freeze-dried dinners are tasty but they can be expensive for a long trip; if you are only going for a few days, I think they are worth the cost and especially like the ones that you can just pour hot water over so that you do not have much to do to clean up. Some recommended food items are: instant oatmeal, pasta, energy bars, gorp, bagels, salami and hard cheese, tortillas with stuffing such as cheese or cooked chicken, hot chocolate or coffee, fruit packages, cereal and powdered milk.

Yippee! Mountain Biking

When the Tahoe Rim Trail was first built, mountain biking was not allowed anywhere on the trail. As time went by and regulations eased, the trail become about 50 percent open to mountain bikers. It is important to understand that the Tahoe Rim Trail is really only suitable for intermediate and advanced riders. Most sections are quite difficult and technical, so riders should make sure they are capable of riding the section before setting out.

The areas closed to bikers include the approximate 50 miles of the route that overlap with the Pacific Crest Trail. Bikes are also forbidden in the wilderness areas: Desolation Wilderness and Mount Rose Wilderness. Also, a section of trail going north from Spooner Summit past Snow Valley Peak to

High above the east shore.

Hobart Road does not allow bikes. Bikes are permitted on the rest of the TRT.

For detailed descriptions of each section of the trail, directions on how to get to trailheads, and special sidebars applying to bikers, refer to individual trail descriptions. A summary of which sections you can or cannot ride on is provided below (these are also shown on the maps).

Section #1: Tahoe City to Brockway—Riding is allowed on the entire section.

Section #2: Brockway to Mount Rose—Mountain biking is allowed between Brockway Summit and the Mount Rose Wilderness Boundary, a distance of about 7 miles. If you start from the Tahoe Meadows end you can ride 4 miles up the dirt road to the radio tower.

Section #3: Tahoe Meadows to Spooner Summit—Mountain biking is allowed between Tahoe Meadows and Hobart Road, which is 14.3

Tim's Top Tips for Mountain Bikers

- 🚲 Ride only where bicycles are permitted.
- 🚲 Wear your helmet.
- 🚲 Speed is your friend: hitting the breaks too hard or going too slowly over a rocky section can send you flying over the bars. With a little speed you can bounce right over the rocks (of course, if you fall, the rule has now changed to "speed is your friend, until it isn't.")
- 🚲 To prevent undue erosion, avoid wet, muddy areas.
- 🚲 Spring and fall temperatures, which would be bearable when you're hiking, get bone-chilling as you cruise downhill at 20 miles an hour. When it's cold, try a warm ski hat under your helmet, warm socks, and lots of layers. Your legs will be pumping so they won't get as cold, but the wind goes right to your neck and through those bike shoes.
- 🚲 Wear bike shoes, bike shorts, and bike shirts; they are well designed to make your ride more enjoyable.
- 🚲 Wear a Camelback or other water-hydration system: mountain biking is strenuous exercise and a water bottle just isn't sufficient on a warm day. Additionally, a Camelback lets you drink without stopping and keeps the water cold throughout the whole ride.
- 🚲 When riding downhill, lift your bottom slightly off the seat, lean back gently, don't grip the handlebars too tightly, and flow down that awesome single track. (Don't forget to yippee!)
- 🚲 Learn how to fix a flat and do minor repairs on your bike; bring a spare inner tube.
- 🚲 Scrapes and cuts are common while biking, carry a small, light First Aid kit in your pack. One good brand is the Optimist by Adventure Medical Kits.

miles (for the section between Tahoe Meadows and Tunnel Creek Road, which is 9.2 miles, mountain biking is allowed only on "Even" days of the month). At Hobart Road, a detour is available down to Marlette Lake and then out to Spooner Lake via North Canyon Road.

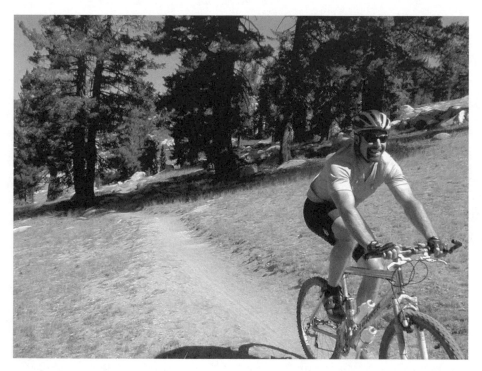

Biker heading for Tunnel Creek.

Section #4: Spooner Summit to Kingsbury Grade—This entire section is open to bikes.

Section #5: Kingsbury Grade to Big Meadow—This entire section is open to bikes.

Section #6: Big Meadow to the Pacific Crest Trail—Bikes are allowed from the Big Meadow Trailhead for about five miles to where the Tahoe Rim Trail meets the Pacific Crest Trail in Meiss Meadows. Bikes are not allowed on the Pacific Crest Trail.

Section #7: Echo Summit to Barker Pass—Bikes are not allowed on this entire section which overlaps with the PCT.

Section #8: Barker Pass to Tahoe City—The first five miles are on the PCT, and as you know by now, bikes are not allowed on the PCT. From Twin Peaks to Tahoe City, bikes are allowed.

Getting Horsey on the TRT

For most horseback riders, the entire Tahoe Rim Trail is a great place to ride. While some equestrians may find a few sections difficult (Desolation Wilderness and an area south of Barker Pass especially), almost all of it is very good for riding. Water is a concern on much of the trail, especially on the east shore. If you are planning on riding the TRT, be sure to read through trail descriptions for detailed information. While on the trail, watch out for other users. Horses are supposed to be given the right of way, but be alert and cautious just the same. Many experts suggest equestrians always wear helmets. Learn the trail ahead of time, and be sure to maintain a comfortable pace for yourself and your horse. Stay on the trail to protect the fragile environment. There are two other issues that equestrians must consider before embarking on a ride along the TRT.

Where To Park the Trailer

Tahoe City—There are two parking locations close to the trailheads. Both can be crowded with narrow access. The first is at the "64 Acres" (Truckee River Access) parking lot located on Highway 89, 0.25 mile south of its intersection with Highway 28 in Tahoe City. From here, you can ride along a paved road for a short distance and then meet the TRT heading toward Page Meadows.

The second Tahoe City parking spot is located at the Fairway Community Center on Fairway Drive, directly across the street from the Tahoe Rim Trail section which goes from Tahoe City to Watson Lake, and then on to Brockway Summit. From the Tahoe City "Y" (the intersection of Highways 89 and 28) go 0.2 mile on Highway 89 toward Truckee and turn right on Fairway Drive. Drive 0.2 mile to the Fairway Community Center on the right. If you park at the "64 Acres" and ride toward Watson Lake, it can be challenging because you must cross a busy bike bridge here, walk on a congested section of bike trail, and then cross Highway 89 to walk 0.2 mile on Fairway Drive.

Brockway Summit—There are two parking areas available here. You can park along the road at the TRT parking area, 0.5 mile east of Brockway Summit, which only has room for a few cars and would require you to unload your horse near a busy road. The second location is 0.2 of a mile past the top of Brockway Summit toward Truckee. On the right is a road leading up to Martis Peak. This is a great spot for horses and from here you can ride your horse up the lightly traveled Martis Peak Road several miles until you meet the TRT.

Mount Rose/Tahoe Meadows—The Tahoe Meadows Trailhead parking lot was designed for horses, but may be congested on a busy day. If no spaces are available, a shoulder is available on the meadow side of the road. After you park, follow the sign toward Brockway Summit or Spooner Summit. If heading toward Brockway Summit from this trailhead, use extreme caution, as you will have to ride parallel to, and then cross, the very busy road to the trailhead.

Spooner Summit—Both trailheads on Spooner Summit have convenient places to park your trailer. It is best to park on the side of the road where you will begin your ride so you do not have to cross Highway 50, a major highway with cars roaring by at high speed.

Kingsbury Grade, North—The north trailhead of Kingsbury Grade has room to park your trailer along this quiet subdivision road.

Kingsbury Grade, South—The large Heavenly Ski Area Stagecoach parking lot should provide plenty of room to park your horse trailer.

Big Meadow—The Big Meadow Parking lot has parking spots designed for horse trailers, but the access is quite narrow. Often the horse-parking spots have been taken by cars in this crowded parking area (if you do not have a horse, give those with horses a break and park in the other spaces if they are available). The parking lot has some winding, sharp turns that can be a challenge. If you are heading toward Freel Peak, you can park along the road near the Grass Lake trailhead and then use this connector trail.

Echo Summit—At the top of the summit on the south side of the road is a large snow park that makes for a great spot to park your trailer. From here, you can ride across the parking lot and head south, or follow the trail north to Lower Echo Lake. There is also parking at Lower Echo Lake, although this can be full to overflowing on summer weekends.

Barker Pass—There is plenty of parking space available at the top of Barker Pass. From here, you can head in either direction on the Tahoe Rim Trail. The paved road up to Barker Pass is a good one, but has a few narrow, twisting turns.

Places To Horse Camp

When looking for a place to camp when you are backpacking, the primary considerations are finding water and a pretty spot. When you have a horse, another concern enters the picture: where do you find grass for your horses without destroying a beautiful meadow? Equestrians should bring their own horse feed instead of relying on unpredictable and fragile grass and meadowlands.

Horses enjoy a break near Dardanelles Lake.

Some of the good camping spots for horses include:

- 🐴 **Watson Lake**
- 🐴 **Ophir Creek**—Go straight at the TRT/Ophir Creek Trail junction to a nice spot near the creek, but out of Tahoe Meadows. You are now on Ophir Creek Trail, but close to the TRT.
- 🐴 **Star Lake**
- 🐴 **Armstrong Pass**—Take the Armstrong Pass connector trail down to the dirt road and a nearby stream. The dry meadow area is known as Horse Meadow.
- 🐴 **Meiss Meadows and the area near Showers Lake**
- 🐴 **Desolation Wilderness**—See permit information in Chapter 4.

- **Ward Canyon, below Twin Peaks**
- **Robie Equestrian Park**—This special 160-acre wilderness equestrian park serves as the staging area for the annual Tevis Cup 100-mile horse ride from Tahoe to Auburn. While not on the Tahoe Rim Trail, the equestrian park is located three miles from Watson Lake, and has two trails with direct access to the TRT. Accessible by vehicle, it is a convenient place for horse camping or setting out for day rides. Livestock water, outhouse facilities, and ample parking are available. The park is open to day-use throughout the summer. Reservations for overnight camping are needed in advance. Contact the Wendell and Inez Robie Foundation at P.O. Box 714, Foresthill, CA 95631, phone (530) 367-4332, or email: robiepk@foothill.net.

Goin' Fishin'

Rainbow trout, brook trout, brown trout, and cutthroat trout are the most common fish in the mountain lakes and streams around Lake Tahoe. In a few lakes, including Lake Tahoe itself, you will also find kokanee salmon and Mackinaw trout (which has edged out the cutthroat in the lake). Most mountain lakes are stocked with fish on a regular basis, although there has been talk of ending the stocking program, especially in wilderness areas. This could greatly affect the mountain fishing experience.

Fishing on the Rim Trail is just like anywhere else: a fishing license is required for anyone over 16 years of age. To obtain a license, contact your local sporting goods store. If you have questions about fishing regulations in California call the California Department of Fish and Game at (916) 358-2900.

In Nevada, call the Nevada Division of Wildlife at (775) 688-1500.

Much of the Tahoe Rim Trail lies along the ridgelines surrounding the Lake Tahoe Basin. It is generally above the lake areas and the major streams that support fish populations. However, there are several locations along the trail that are good for fishing, and a number of spur trails to take you to good fishing sites. In general, since most of the lakes and streams are above the west shore, that is where the best fishing opportunities are.

Since half the fun of fishing is discovering your own secret hole, I am only going to reveal the more popular places below.

Desolation Wilderness/Western Rim—The area between Echo Lakes and Barker Pass has an abundance of fishable lakes. Explore the area and you will find the best spots to fish.

Truckee River—In Tahoe City the TRT meets the Truckee River, a popular fishing spot. During summer months this area is also popular with rafters. It is best to fish in early morning or late afternoon, or you may catch a big raft instead of a trout.

North Shore—Watson Lake, which is a fairly shallow lake, is pretty much your only choice in this area. Two other lakes in the area, Gray Lake and Mud Lake, do not have fish and are sometimes not even lakes.

East Shore—Only a few lakes of any size exist on the east shore. Close to the trail and right off the highway is Spooner Lake, a catch-and-release fishing area only. Marlette Lake is used for spawning, so fishing is not allowed. Because the shallow Twin Lakes often dry up in late season, they lack fish, but Star Lake, at the base of Jobs Sister, has trout.

South Shore/Meiss Meadows Areas—In this area, the Upper Truckee River, Meiss Lake, Dardanelles Lake, Round Lake, and Showers Lake provide opportunities for fishing. In recent years Tahoe's native fish, the Lahontan cutthroat, has been reintroduced to these waters.

The best way to make sure that Tahoe area waterways continue to have fish is to practice the catch-and-release fishing technique. Create barbless hooks by smashing the barb on your hook with a pair of pliers. Once you catch the fish, treat them gently. Remove the hook while the fish is still in the water and release it back into the environment to where it belongs. If you are camping and really would enjoy a fish dinner, go ahead, but be sure to only take the fish you will eat (and don't clean the fish in the nearest lake or stream).

For more details about fishing in the Sierra, refer to *Sierra Trout Guide* by Ralph Cutter, published by Amato Publications. It provides a list of every lake in the Sierra and what kind of fish may be found there. Or check out Ralph's website at www.flyline.com. Another informative source is the *Desolation Wilderness Fishing Guide* by Jerome Yesavage, also published by Amato. Wilderness Press distributes both books; you can reach them at (800) 443-7227.

Kids Like to Hike . . . Some Kids. . . Sometimes . . . and, Not Too Far

The Tahoe Rim Trail is a challenging trail for grown-ups because it traverses terrain that has lots of elevation gain. Much of the trail is simply not suitable for younger children. There are, however, a few great destinations for family outings. Here are a few suggestions on my favorite places to take chil-

Three amigas overlooking Ward Canyon.

dren. The complete route descriptions are in Chapter 6.

Mount Rose/Tahoe Meadows Area—Near the top of the Mount Rose Highway at Tahoe Meadows, the Tahoe Rim Trail has two trailheads and an interpretive trail. All three provide an opportunity for kids to learn about and enjoy the mountains. Each of these trailheads is located above 8000 feet, about 7.5 miles up Highway 431 from the intersection of Highway 28 and Highway 431 in Incline Village. They are all in the same vicinity or across the street from each other.

Tahoe Meadows Interpretative Trail—If you are coming from Incline Village, on Highway 431, you will see a parking area and a building set down below the road on the right hand side after about 7.5 miles. This marks a trail, which has been built to be wheelchair and stroller accessible, a very easy

1.3-mile loop. The trail starts on the eastern edge of the lower parking area and winds through the meadow. It is a great spot for early summer wild-flowers and a place where the little ones can stretch their legs. This is the easiest segment of the Tahoe Rim Trail and would be suitable for very young children.

Tahoe Meadows to Spooner Summit—This hike starts from the western edge of the same parking lot as described just above. First, the trail traverses Tahoe Meadows and passes a display of wildflow-ers, a few small streams, and the larger Ophir Creek —a playground for kids. Once you have crossed the meadow, the trail levels out and heads uphill, not too steeply, to the top of a saddle located at 1.7 miles from the trailhead. From the saddle, the trail levels off again and remains mostly level for several miles with only a few gentle up and down passages. The views of the lake are incredible and there are numerous flat rock "armchairs" inviting you to enjoy your lunch or a snack. Walk as far as you want and then turn around. This area is also a great spot for someone who is learning how to snowshoe or ski cross-country.

Tahoe Meadows to Brockway Summit—From Incline Village, on Highway 431, drive past the main Tahoe Meadows trailhead on your right and go another 0.4 mile. You reach a gated Forest Ser-vice road on your left. Here you can park along the shoulder of the highway near the road as long as you do not block its access. For your family outing, hike up the dirt road. Lake Tahoe, Incline Lake, Tahoe Meadows, and the mountains around the lake come into view. The first 1.5 miles are a steady but gentle climb and give you splendid panoramas along the way. The trail levels off eventually for about a mile as you head north. At 2.5 miles from the trailhead, you reach a meadow and a small unnamed pond, called Snow Pond or Frog Pond by locals. Depending on the age and attitude of your children, you may be able to continue toward the radio tower (another much steeper 1.5 miles), but this is also a good place to turn around. The meadow is a quiet place for a picnic, where the kids can run around in the grass. Just to the east of the pond is a junction with a trail leading to Mount Rose. After an easy first mile or so, this trail becomes strenuous. The first part of it provides access to some beautiful summertime wildflower displays.

Big Meadow Area—Drive 5.3 miles south of Meyers on Highway 89 to the Tahoe Rim Trail Big Meadow Trailhead. This trail heads northeast toward Kingsbury Grade, or south 5 miles to where the Tahoe Rim Trail intersects the Pacific Crest Trail. If your children are hearty, they may enjoy the hike south where, after about 3 miles and approximately 800 feet of elevation gain, you will reach Round Lake. Along the way, you will traverse through lovely Big Meadow. You will also encounter some huge volcanic rock formations. The lake itself is a great respite for the kids. (You could also take the spur trail to Dardanelles Lake, a beautiful lake located 3.4 miles from the trailhead).

Echo Lakes Area—At Lower Echo Lake (see directions in Chapter 6, Section 7), you will find a store, a small marina, and a large parking facility. From the lake, your trail is the Tahoe Rim Trail, Tahoe-Yosemite Trail, and the Pacific Crest Trail all combined; it heads north. The first 2.5 miles go along the Lower and Upper Echo Lakes and provide great views of the lakes. This trail has some fun up-and-down passages and rocky scrambles, perfect for any 10 year old.

At the end of 2.5 miles, you can continue on the trail, turn around, or take the Echo Lakes Water

Taxi back to the Echo Lakes parking lot. The taxi is a small boat that crosses back and forth across the lakes. It only operates seasonally, so be sure to check ahead for taxi times and to make sure it is running. Late in the summer the lake level drops too low to allow passage for the taxi between Lower and Upper Echo Lakes. For more information about the Echo Lakes Water Taxi, contact Echo Chalet at (530) 659-7207.

Another option is to take the taxi to the end of the two lakes and cut out 2.5 miles of a trip to Lake of the Woods or Lake Aloha. If you take the water taxi, it is only about 3 miles to Lake of the Woods, and 3.5 miles to the eastern edge of Lake Aloha. I found Lake Aloha to be a perfect spot to take my child on a backpacking trip. Be prepared for a hearty climb of about 1000 feet through rocky terrain.

Page Meadows Area—The Page Meadows area can be approached from several different directions and is an excellent and easy place to take the kids on a hike. Probably the easiest way into the area is through the back of the Talmont Estates/Twin Peaks subdivision. Take Highway 89 south about 2 miles from Tahoe City. Turn right on Pine Avenue. In about 0.2 mile, turn right on Tahoe Park Heights. Follow Tahoe Park Heights to the top of the hill and then take Big Pine, the middle of three roads. Continue on Big Pine for about 0.25 mile to Silvertip Drive where you turn left. Follow Silvertip to the end of the road and park where you see a sign that reads: SKI PARKING. A dirt road heads west from the end of the road. Follow it down the hill straight ahead until you pass a sharp left-hand turn. Just after the turn, a single-track trail heads off to the right and arrives at the first meadow in about 100 yards. Follow along the edge of the meadow until you see a trail heading left (west) through the

81

meadow. From here you can start exploring. The trail goes by several big meadows. The meadows provide tremendous mountain views, great wildflowers in the summer, and lots of aspen trees making it prime for fall colors. Bring a picnic lunch and a Frisbee and have at it with the kids. Avoid trampling in the fragile meadow area, at least until late summer or fall when the area has had a chance to dry out.

Ward Canyon Area—On Highway 89, drive 2.4 miles south of Tahoe City, past Sunnyside Resort to Pineland Drive on the right. In 0.4 mile this becomes Twin Peaks Drive. Stay on the left at the Y and in about 0.1 mile the road becomes Ward Creek Boulevard. Take this about 1.5 miles to a TAHOE RIM TRAIL sign on your left where the trail begins. Follow the old road as it parallels the largely unseen Ward Creek for the next three miles. Go as far as you want and then turn around. The trail eventually leads rather steeply up to Twin Peaks, but that would be a long haul for the little ones. The first three miles, however, are just a gentle uphill with lots of wildflowers in season, Ward Creek nearby, and wonderful views of the Sierra crest above.

What About Fido?

While dogs are allowed on much of the Tahoe Rim Trail, restrictions do apply at several state parks, including Lake Tahoe Nevada State Park. In fact, regulations governing dogs on trails completely depend on what county you are passing through. It is your responsibility to know what the specific regulations are under each county's jurisdiction. In general, it is best to leave the pups at home or, at least, keep them on a leash. Dogs off leash chase and interfere with wildlife, and trample the understory of forests. Your chances of encountering wild creatures will increase and you'll have the satisfaction of knowing that you are limiting your impact on the trail. If you do hike with your pooch, be sure to have him or her on a leash or under voice command at all times. Dogs jumping on other hikers, chasing mountain bikers, running beyond your sight line, or harassing horses are a big no-no. If you have a well trained, on-leash animal that doesn't go after every squirrel or chase every lizard, by all means take him or her along.

Some dogs love to take a dip in Round Lake.

Locator Map for Tahoe Rim Trail

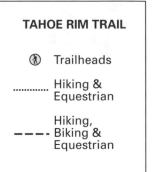

TAHOE RIM TRAIL

🚶 Trailheads

············· Hiking & Equestrian

– – – – Hiking, Biking & Equestrian

CHAPTER SIX

Trail Descriptions

Throughout these trail descriptions, mileages are given from point-to-point. Mileage figures were based on several sources; the primary sources for the maps you see in this book are Tom Harrison's "Lake Tahoe Recreation Map," which has been enhanced with information generously provided by Jeffrey P. Schaffer, whose *Tahoe Sierra* and *Pacific Crest Trail: Northern California* set the standard for guidebooks in this area. These figures will give you distances between certain locations. However, you should realize that when it says 0.9 mile, another source might report it as 1.1 mile. If this difference really bothers you, perhaps you need to relax a bit. I have found the best way to relax is to spend time walking in the woods. For your convenience, a mileage chart for the Tahoe Rim Trail appears in Appendix A.

Before each description, I recommend when the section can be hiked without encountering large amounts of snow. These dates are estimates based on an "average snow year," but in reality there is no such thing as an *average* year. It either snows more than average or less than average. The dates should give you a rough idea of when you can hike. If it has been an especially mild winter and a warm spring, you could expect to hike the trail sooner than the dates stated here. Refer to Chapter 4 on weather for more detail on snow seasons.

Finally, the Tahoe Rim Trail is constantly evolving. Minor trail changes for maintenance and realignment are being planned and implemented on a regular basis. Although this book attempts to be up-to-date, changes to the trail may have been made since this book was published. For more information on any recent changes to the trail, contact the Tahoe Rim Trail Association at (775) 298-0012.

Legend for Maps in Trail Descriptions

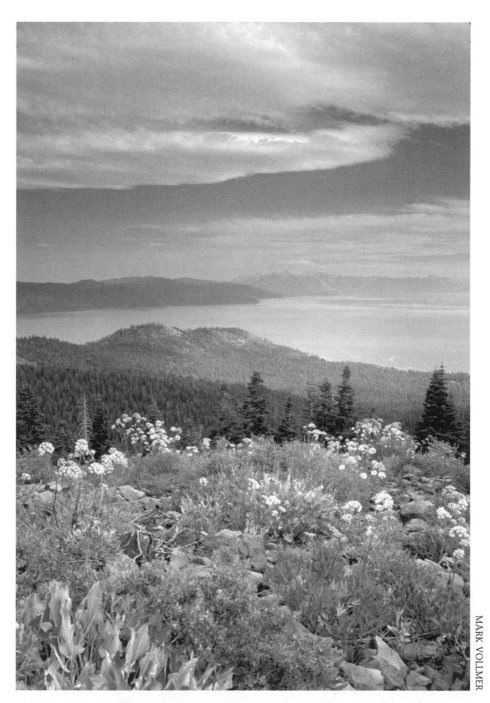

*View of Lake Tahoe from viewpoint
east of Brockway Summit.*

87

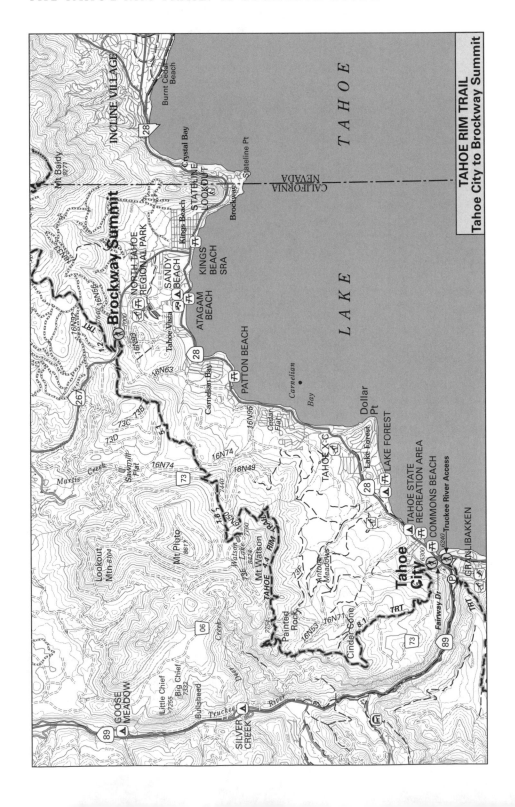

TAHOE RIM TRAIL
Tahoe City to Brockway Summit

Tahoe City to Brockway Summit
(19.2 miles)

Difficulty—This section is strenuous. It is long and requires a good deal of climbing, and can be quite hot in the summer when it is also mostly waterless. During the first 2 miles, sharp rocks on the trail might be hard on the feet.

Best Seasons—While portions of the trail at lower elevations can be utilized from late May to early November, higher elevation areas keep the snow until later. The snow melts first along the first several miles north of Tahoe City.

Highlights—This section includes a pleasant open forest with a wide variety of plants. Much of the area has been extensively logged over the years, so you will see mostly smaller, newer growth trees. Views of the lake are found in several locations. You can also enjoy mountain views of Twin Peaks, Alpine Meadows, and Squaw Valley from several places along the trail. Watson Lake, while not the most beautiful lake along the Tahoe Rim Trail, is a pleasant shallow lake nestled among the trees you will find two-thirds of the way through your hike.

Heads Up!—This is a long stretch and water is in short supply. No year-round water sources exist except for Watson Lake located 12.5 miles from Tahoe City and 6.7 miles from Brockway Summit. Watson Lake is shallow and has water that does not look enticing to drink. (These days, you should treat water from even the most sparkling lakes.) A stream east of Watson Lake may be available in the early season. Bring lots of water if you're hiking this section! With many road crossings and much

89

Looking west towards Alpine Meadows, Squaw Valley and the Pacific Crest.

off-highway-vehicle (OHV) use, don't be surprised to hear or see cars close to the trail. For mountain bikers, the rocky terrain can be challenging, even frustrating. This section is not recommended for beginner riders.

Getting There, Tahoe City to Brockway—From the Tahoe City "Y" at the intersection of Highways 89 and 28, go 0.2 mile west on Highway 89 toward Truckee. Just past a gas station (a Chevron at the time this book is published), turn right on Fairway Drive. Drive another 0.2 mile to a parking lot and the Fairway Community Center on the right. If this parking lot is full, you can park (weekends only) at the Tahoe City Public Utility District offices about 0.1 mile back toward Highway 89. Your trailhead is across the street from the center.

Getting There, Brockway to Tahoe City—From the intersection of Highway 28 and Highway 267 in

Kings Beach, drive 2.75 miles north on Highway 267 to the TRT trailhead. Look carefully—it is easy to miss. Parking is available at the road pullout on the left, at 0.5 mile before Brockway Summit. The trail starts right at the downhill edge of the parking area. If you plan on mountain biking this section, it is best to head south from Brockway Summit toward Tahoe City, although either direction will challenge you with steep, rocky terrain that includes technically challenging sections.

Trail Description

From the Tahoe City trailhead, the trail starts out as a moderate 10% uphill grade and passes through thick sections of manzanita and patches of squaw carpet, and through a forest of white fir, Jeffrey pine, sugar pine, and incense-cedar trees. After about 0.7 mile you cross a dirt road; for a little history lesson, detour right and climb steeply uphill about 100 yards and then turn right. You will see a white cross that sits above Tahoe City. For the story, read the sidebar below.

Sidetrip: Boyle's Last Ride

According to local legend, William Boyle was an easy-going codger with a dry sense of humor who lived in Tahoe City in the early 20th Century. He once asked his drinking buddies to bury him above the town so he could keep an eye on them. True to their word, his friends dragged Boyle up the hill on a sled and buried him above Tahoe City on February 4, 1912. Shortly afterward, the cross was erected at the site. Photos taken at that time period show a clear, treeless view down to the lake. Now, however, trees and brush have grown so thickly that much of the view from the cross has been obscured.

91

Back on the Tahoe Rim Trail several lake views open up through the trees as you head steadily uphill over very rocky terrain. You are traversing through a fairly thick, mixed forest of Jeffrey pine, white fir, and incense-cedar. About 2.25 miles in from the trailhead you see an expansive view to the west of the Twin Peaks ridgeline and Squaw Valley. The climb has become easier and the trail more rocky, with fewer trees on the meager soil. About 0.3 mile past the view, you make the first of many crossings of a major dirt road that locals call the Fiberboard Freeway (alias Road 16N73, Forest Route 73), after the company that once was the principal landholder in the area. The term "freeway" is derived from the fact that this wide gravel road is the main backcountry route linking Tahoe City and Brockway Summit (and via another connection, Truckee). After crossing the road, continue gently uphill over rocky terrain for another 0.5 mile to a viewpoint on top of some lava rocks, about 3.4 miles from the trailhead. Walk carefully over boulders to the high point, which lies clearly about 100 yards east, to see stunning views of Lake Tahoe to the southeast, and Mt. Watson to the northeast.

The trail now turns west and ascends gently across the rocky terrain and sparse forest, until at about 4.1 miles from the trailhead you pass the dark-red volcanic rock known as the Cinder Cone on the right. Longtime Tahoe locals will tell you that this cinder-cone area was the repository for Tahoe City sewer water before the treatment plant was built in Truckee in the 1970s. Does that change your mind about where you planned to stop for lunch? As the trail skirts the Cinder Cone you will see the remnants of an old fence. (See sidetrip to Cinder Cone, next page.)

As you continue on the trail, which curves southwest, you will pass the Cinder Cone and soon

Sidetrip: Cinder Cone

If you would like to see the Cinder Cone itself and avoid a bit of walking, leave the trail and walk northwest beyond the fencing. You'll be on the mostly flat, red surface of the Cinder Cone. The lack of plant growth and evidence of filled-in ditches clearly show that the site was once impacted by human use. Continue northwest toward the ridge. In less than 0.25 mile you will intersect the Tahoe Rim Trail.

reach the east rim of the Truckee River canyon. From here you get stunning views west into Alpine Meadows valley, as well as southwest to Ward Canyon in the distance to the left. Finally, after the long meander west around the cone, the trail heads north for 0.5 mile and then descends rather steeply (those who crossed the Cinder Cone rejoin the trail before this downhill). A small north-facing section in thick forest here may hold a remaining patch of the previous winter's snow. Soon, you reach an open saddle at the end of a little-used dirt road, 5.0 miles from the trailhead, and then begin heading gently uphill through an open forest of fir trees and manzanita. Quickly the trail proceeds downhill and the forest becomes thicker and your hike shadier.

Like most of the northern and western shores of Lake Tahoe, this area has been heavily logged in the past. The most extensive logging occurred in the late 1800s when much of the Tahoe Basin was logged to make braces in the silver mines of nearby Virginia City to keep them from collapsing (as well as for lumber and fuel). Loggers at that time focused on the best trees for their purposes—the pine trees, especially the majestic sugar pine—and left most of the fir trees. During an extended wet period, the red and white firs took over the territory from the more drought- and disease-resistant

93

Jeffrey and sugar pines, creating an unnaturally dense forest of firs primarily. If nature had been allowed to revert to its own natural process, periodic forest fires would have thinned the population of fir. Instead, the federal and state governments, under heavy pressure to prevent forest fires and to limit tree cutting, had a policy of preventing major forest fires by putting out all fires as quickly as possible. In the short-term this policy saved the forest, but it led to a denser forest, and increased the likelihood of a catastrophic fire. We now know that this historic policy excluded the ecological role of frequent natural fires. Adding to the danger, in the early 1990s when annual precipitation was below normal for several years in a row, many trees died when they were unable to resist the debilitating impact of the bark beetle. Expansive stands of dead trees in an overly thick forest are a recipe for disaster. The National Forest Service and both the Nevada and California State Park Departments began an aggressive effort of salvage logging and controlled burning to reduce the danger. As you walk or ride on the Tahoe Rim Trail, you may see evidence of this effort in many locations in the form of brush piles waiting to be burned and stumps from recent logging.

About 1 mile past the last dirt road, you cross another dirt road. (See sidetrip to "The Wall," next page.) This one is in a dry gully above the headwaters of Burton Creek. Those desperate for water can head 0.75 mile southeast down the road to its end at the Fiberboard Freeway (Forest Route 73). Turn left there and head briefly north to the creek.

To continue on the TRT, you will cross this second dirt road to enter prime mountain-biking terrain. The amount of trail traffic will increase dramatically. The trail here is part of a network of trails providing great biking opportunities out of

Sidetrip: "The Wall"

A left turn here would quickly take you 300 yards northwest to a minor saddle and the start of a steep downhill, known as "The Wall" by mountain-biking enthusiasts. It leads to the Western States Trail and in a few steep downhill miles to the bike trail at the bridge across the Truckee River between Squaw Valley and Alpine Meadows. The bike trail leads back to Tahoe City and the beginning of the TRT; this makes a nice loop.

Tahoe City and the Tahoe Cross-Country Ski Area located in the Highlands subdivision. The next stage is a mostly moderate climb through soft volcanic dirt and mixed forest 0.9 mile to the east edge of Painted Rock (7754'). Along the way you'll pass some impressive volcanic boulders. After the climb to Painted Rock, you're rewarded with two good viewpoints: one offers a panorama southeast toward Lake Tahoe; another spot a little farther on gives you an awe-inspiring view into Squaw Valley backed by the Sierra crest.

After all the uphill work you have done in the last 7 miles, you get a break with a mostly shady descent (or if on a bike, a really fun downhill) to another crossing of the Fiberboard Freeway at about 8 miles from the Tahoe City trailhead. Here, usually on the first Sunday in March, The Great Ski Race passes this point on its way to Truckee. This 30-kilometer cross-country ski race, from the Tahoe Cross Country Ski Area on Dollar Hill to Truckee, attracts up to a thousand people, making it one of the biggest cross-country ski events in the western United States. For the next 0.8 mile you cover a smooth, gentle incline over hard-packed sandy soils (mountain bikers should ride it back down to know one of the best biking stretches on the whole TRT). Where the trail levels off and runs into an old

95

Sidetrip: Mt. Watson

A left turn at the Fiberboard Freeway would take you back to Tahoe City, while a right turn would take you to Truckee, Brockway Summit or to the top of Mt. Watson. Should you want to climb or ride to Mt. Watson, follow the Freeway uphill from where it meets the dirt road for 0.7 mile to a junction with a major dirt road that turns sharply right (southeast). Turn onto this road and follow it for 1 mile on a 640-foot ascent to the top of Mt. Watson (8424'). Views from the top are glorious; you can see most of Lake Tahoe and its surrounding mountains as well as Squaw Valley and Alpine Meadows to the west.

narrow dirt road, a left turn will take you 100 yards north to the Fiberboard Freeway.

Just south of the Fiberboard Freeway, take the TRT; it turns right and follows an old abandoned dirt road, now overgrown with manzanita and tobacco brush. This gentle downhill stretch continues 1.6 miles before a left turn heads you back uphill. You now wind uphill, northeast, between lava boulders and cliffs for the next 0.75 mile to a wonderful stopping place among several especially large boulders, with enticing views of the lake to the south between the boulders. Beyond the viewpoint, the trail levels off and turns right before it reaches another junction, 1 mile short of Watson Lake. (A left turn here would take you steeply uphill to the top of Mt. Watson.)

Continue straight ahead on the TRT on a moderately steep downhill towards Watson Lake. Just before the lake, you reach a gravel road; turn left on this road and follow it uphill. In a short distance, the TRT takes off to the right and skirts the east shore of Watson Lake. While little Watson Lake is pleasant enough, it is shallow, surrounded by trees, and visited by numerous mosquitoes. It can also be heavily used in the summer since it is the only lake between Brockway Summit and Tahoe City, and accessible by car along a paved and gravel road. At all times be sure to filter water at Watson Lake if you feel you may need more water before the end of the route.

After you pass the lake, with 12.5 miles under your belt and 6.7 miles to go, the TRT heads about 0.25 mile north to a shallow gully. The trail now descends gently 1.25 miles east through beautiful wildflower meadows and forested areas, to a road, down which you can head 0.3 mile to usually reliable Watson Creek. You pass several small seep streams that provide water until mid-summer. Since these are the last water sources along this section, take advantage of the opportunity if it's still available. Just 0.25 mile east beyond the road, a short (90 yards) spur trail leads off to the right to a large rock pile with another pretty view of Lake Tahoe, specifically Carnelian Bay. Enjoy the view— it's the last full lake view you'll get before reaching the Brockway Summit trailhead in about 4.5 miles.

The trail turns north and in 0.8 mile switchbacks down through a thick forest of white fir and Jeffrey pine to a crossing of Forest Route 74, and 100 yards farther crosses Forest Route 75. After a gentle descent northeast for about two-thirds of a mile, you cross another road, then traverse about 200 yards to yet another. Now you have a fairly gentle climb for 1 mile as the trail takes you through manzanita and chinquapin before it crosses Forest Service Road 73 (Fiberboard Freeway). There is still more climbing for 1.3 mile until you cross the Fiberboard Freeway one more time. The next 0.7 mile gently descends to the trailhead, located on the same side of Highway 267. At this point, you are about 0.5 mile east of Brockway Summit.

TAHOE RIM TRAIL
Brockway to Tahoe Meadows

Brockway Summit to
Tahoe Meadows (18.9 miles)

Difficulty—With much of this section of the trail rising above 9,000' and some of it over 10,000' in elevation, it is relatively strenuous, especially considering you start at around 7000'. If you are day-hiking this section, it might be easier to begin from the Tahoe Meadows side and hike to Brockway Summit, where your starting elevation would be approximately 8800'. As they say, 1800 feet here and 1800 feet there and eventually you are talking about some real elevation gain.

Best Seasons—The entire trail can be hiked between late July and mid-October. The first 5 miles from the Brockway end can be hiked as early as June, but most of the trail is not free of snow until mid-July. The highest sections of the trail are among the first places to be covered with snow in the fall.

Highlights—The middle part of this trail section is mostly exposed, south-facing volcanic slopes with sandy soils. This wide expanse at a high altitude features tremendous panoramic views of the lake and a wonderful feeling of remoteness. Two small lakes are found on the trail, or close to it: small Mud Lake and Gray Lake, a prettier, knee-deep lake that is 0.5 mile off the Rim Trail via an access trail.

Heads Up!—Since much of this hike is at high altitude, the air is quite thin, which can cause problems for those unaccustomed to high altitudes. If you feel faint, it may be due to reduced oxygen levels rather than the beauty of the views. Much of the trail is exposed to cold and wind, or to the hot sun.

The first 5 miles can be tedious; the last 4 miles are on a dirt road; but the middle 10 miles are a wonderful high-altitude experience. Though water can be collected from several seasonal streams, and from Gray Lake and usually from Mud Lake, the supply is severely limited. A small seasonal spring exists about 50 feet below where the TRT meets the old Western States Trail (now abandoned) after Mud Lake. Gray Lake is about 0.5 mile downhill from a saddle just past Mud Lake, and Mud Lake itself lives up to its name by becoming a mud puddle by late summer. About 2.5 miles from the end of the trail, you'll find a small pond (known as both Snow Pond and Frog Pond) across from the trail to Mount Rose.

Tips for Mountain Bikers—If you are looking for a good section of the Tahoe Rim Trail to ride, this is probably not the one to choose. Please do *not* ride in the portion of this trail that does not allow bikes! The soil is quite fragile and easily damaged.

From the Brockway Summit side, bikes are allowed for the first 7.6 miles. It begins with a steady and sometimes steep climb of 4.3 miles to a major gravel road. From here you can take a left turn and head back to the highway on the road. On the way back to the highway, you will pass Martis Peak Road which will take you up to the Martis Peak Fire Lookout, with spectacular views to the north. Back on the TRT you could turn right and ride another mile, but it gets quite steep and technical and may not be worth the effort.

From the Mount Rose/Tahoe Meadows end of this section of the TRT, the first 4 miles are open to bike riders, but it is all on a rocky dirt road that gets quite steep near the top. You will come to a radio tower. Here you must turn around and bounce back down the road to the highway.

Getting There, Brockway to Mount Rose Highway (Tahoe Meadows)—From the intersection of Highway 28 and Highway 267 in Kings Beach, drive 2.75 miles northwest up Highway 267 toward Brockway Summit to the Tahoe Rim Trail trailhead. At this point, you will see a parking pullout on the left and a steep dirt road on the right (Forest Service Road 16N56). Park on either side but this trailhead is on the right, or uphill side. If you reach Brockway Summit at the top of the hill you have gone 0.5 mile too far.

Getting There, Mount Rose Highway (to Brockway Summit)—Take Highway 431 (Mount Rose Highway) to Tahoe Meadows, then on to a closed, gated road branching left just before Mount Rose Summit. This road is on the uphill side of Highway 431. You'll see a small building at 7.7 miles from the intersection of Highway 28 and 431 in Incline Village. Park alongside the road, or downhill 0.4 mile at the Tahoe Meadows trailhead parking area. The trail route is on the dirt road behind the gate and a trailhead sign. From Reno, this trailhead is found about 0.3 mile after the highway tops Mount Rose Summit.

Trail Description

From the Brockway trailhead, cross the busy road carefully if you are parked on the south side of Highway 267, and follow the dirt road uphill (east) 100 yards to the trail and trailhead sign. The trail leads off to the left into the trees. This first section is no-nonsense, fairly steep, with occasional views of the lake as you switchback through a thick forest of newer growth Jeffrey pines and white firs. Walk quickly to escape the drone of automobile traffic from the road below. After about 0.5 mile, the views get better as you pass through an area of manzanita and squaw carpet. In early summer you will

101

also encounter numerous wildflowers. Listen closely you may hear the mating call of a blue grouse. (Sounds like a bass drum, "brmmmmm, brmm-mmm, brmmmmm.")

After about 1 mile of steady climbing, you reach a junction at 1.2 miles from the trailhead.

Sidetrip: View from a Rock

On your left is a short spur trail which heads 0.3 miles up to a pile of rocks that look as though they were part of a set for "The Flintstones." From atop the rocks, you get great lake views to the south, and mountain views to the north and west.

The TRT continues straight ahead on a ridge, descending briefly before leveling off. Here it becomes more open; you will see fewer trees in a more scattered pattern, along with mule ears, a very common plant with large leaves and large yellow flowers. About 0.7 mile past the spur trail, you cross a gravel road (16N33) about 150 yards east of its junction with the paved Martis Peak Road. You start heading up again gently, before another short downhill to a small grassy opening with early summer flowers and a streamlet providing water in the springtime.

Next, head steeply up again through a forest that is transitioning from Jeffrey pines and white firs to the higher-altitude lodgepole pines and red firs. The air is thick with the pungent cinnamon aroma of tobacco brush. Your climb eases and you come out of the forest into a huge field of equally aromatic mule ears. Continuing uphill you leave the thick forest and the scenery changes dramatically. You reach an open rock pile, almost 4 miles from the trailhead that hosts dramatic views to the south of Lake Tahoe. Looking to the south across the lake, you can see (clockwise from east to west) Snow Valley Peak (9914'), the highest peak above the east shore; Jobs Sister (10,823'); Freel Peak (10,881'); South Lake Tahoe; Mt. Tallac (9735'); Desolation Wilderness and the Crystal Range; Twin Peaks (8878') above the west shore; and finally Squaw Valley and Northstar. Freel Peak and Jobs Sister are the two highest peaks in the Tahoe Basin. If you continue on the TRT for another 64 miles you will walk just below Freel Peak as you cross a saddle at 9730'. If you enjoy sitting in the sunshine while eating your lunch, this south-facing spot may be just the spot. On September 22, 2001, this view-point was the location for the official opening dedication ceremony for the Tahoe Rim Trail.

Lake Tahoe from above Kings Beach, looking south to Mt. Tallac.

When you can drag yourself away from the panoramic views of the lake, continue up rocky terrain along the edge of a ridge. You will have a clear view of Mt. Baldy to the east, and the beautiful aspen groves along its flanks. With Mt. Baldy as

103

your goal, you pass a rocky viewpoint to your right, and a field full of mule ears to your left, before heading back into the woods again briefly before reaching a major dirt road at 4.3 miles in from your trailhead.

Sidetrip: Martis Peak Lookout

A left turn on this dirt road will take you to the Martis Peak (8742') lookout. To get there go 0.2 mile and then turn right and take the paved road 0.7 mile up to the lookout at 8656'. From here you will see excellent views of most of Lake Tahoe and the crest that rims it to the south, and to the north, most of the lands from the Donner Pass and Lake environs east into western Nevada.

The TRT turns to the right and follows the dusty road about 0.25 mile north to a fork. Keep left and gently ascend 300 yards north to a trailhead with parking for several vehicles. You have now reached a part of the old Western States Trail, also known as the Capital-to-Capital Trail because it once linked Carson City (the capital of Nevada) with Sacramento (the capital of California). The trail starts east through forest and alternating open rocky sections and in 0.5 mile reaches a saddle with views north. The tree composition is transitioning again with more red firs and occasional junipers, western white pines, and the first hemlocks that you will see on this section. Your climb becomes steeper as you switchback 0.3 mile up to a ridgeline that has views into a large U-shaped valley, the drainage area for Juniper Creek, which empties into the Truckee River. After about a 300-yard traverse southeast on the ridgeline, the trail angles south for a 0.4-mile traverse of gentle slopes to a road; from here, the trail ascends 0.2 miles south to the road's end and the resumption of trail tread. In

less than 0.5 mile you climb first moderately southeast, then moderately northeast up to the ridgeline.
There's a great view here, but even more superlative
ones lie ahead. Just 0.2 mile south you reach a low
rock pile immediately west of the trail. This has
dramatic views of the lake to the south, and mountains to the west and east. In addition, there are
great views to the north in which you can see Castle
Peak, Donner Lake, the town of Truckee, and Boca
and Stampede Reservoirs.

From this view, you are now about 6.8 miles
from the Brockway Summit trailhead. The TRT goes
briefly east to the ridgeline, where you cross into
Nevada. (This is a good place to turn around if you
are on a bike.) As the trees get smaller and fewer,
and you get higher, now above 9000', the ridgeline
area opens up. Only the hardiest trees, such as
lodgepole pine, western white pine and whitebark
pine grow here. On the north-facing slopes below,
and also east of you, snow may last well into the
summer. After climbing moderately southeast 0.5
mile up the ridgeline, the TRT angles northeast, traversing just under a minor summit on a high ridge,
which is 9271' Mt. Baldy. Just past it, you enter the
Mount Rose Wilderness. At about 7.6 miles from
the trailhead, this is the end of the section of trail
permissible to mountain bikes. *Bike riding is not allowed in the wilderness.* (A better place to turn around
would have been the viewpoint you just passed, or
where the trail met the dirt road, at 4.3 miles from
the Brockway trailhead).

Now you traverse the side of an open south-
east-facing slope with incredible expansive views to
the south and east of Lake Tahoe, Incline Village
and beyond. For the next 2 miles, with the exception of a brief uphill foray into the forest, you walk
beneath a volcanic ridge eastward on a gentle ascent over wonderful light brown sandy soil through
huge open fields of mule ears. Views of the lake are

105

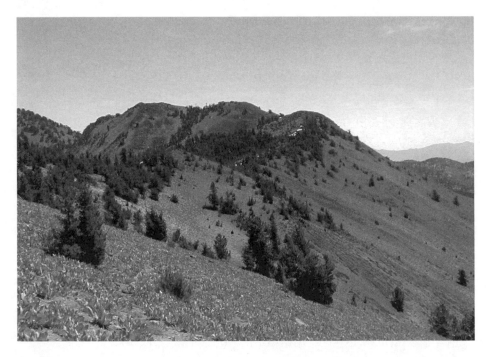

Looking toward Rose Knob Peak.

truly glorious with almost the entire lake displayed before you. It is a real highlight of the Tahoe Rim Trail, and considering how far you are from either the Tahoe Meadows or Brockway trailheads, you may even have it all to yourself.

About midway on your northeast traverse you pass just beneath a steep-sided 9499' summit, behind which lies unseen, flat-topped Rifle Peak. In 0.5 mile you traverse beneath pyramidal Rose Knob, then in another 0.5 mile reach a junction. You are now about 9.8 miles from the Brockway Summit trailhead. Here the old Western States Trail forks left, goes 30 yards to the ridgeline, follows its sometimes snowy north-facing slopes 0.25 mile east, then makes a meandering, moderate descent 0.6 mile northeast down to clear, but knee-deep Gray Lake, which has campsites above its north shore. The TRT, however, stays high and continues straight ahead, east across south-facing slopes toward Rose Knob Peak (9710'), an impressive pile of volcanic rock with three distinct pointy peaks. After a 0.5 mile traverse across slopes, the TRT crosses a saddle with clusters of whitebark pines, then soon climbs 0.25 mile southeast, where it passes beneath the southernmost summit of Rose Knob Peak. Then the trail rounds the bend and travels northeast across talus on the south-facing side of the mountain.

This rocky section was one of the last parts of the trail to be completed, and one of the most difficult to build. The trail builders have constructed formidable rock walls and created a fairly smooth trail through the talus field. As you go around the mountain you will once again enjoy magnificent views of almost the entire lake. After a 0.3-mile traverse across mostly talus, the trail angles north and contours over to a saddle above Mud Lake; this stretch has a few scattered mountain hemlocks. At the east edge of the saddle is a junction, about 11.2 miles from the Brockway Summit trailhead and 7.7 miles from the Mount Rose trailhead.

Sidetrip: Gray Lake

To the left (north) of the TRT, the old Western States Trail makes a steep downhill grade of about 0.5 mile to Gray Lake, a small lake surrounded by grasses and wildflowers. Why not visit Mud Lake, which is just below us to the right? Here's why: Mud Lake lives up to its name. In late summer it gets quite small before sometimes disappearing altogether. Gray Lake may be the only lake easily accessible and worth visiting on this section of trail. A charming streamlet drops down through the rocks into the southern edge of the lake. While in early and mid-summer the lake can be a haven for mosquitoes, in the fall it is a pleasant and quiet place to relax. At 9043' this lake with marshy surroundings is quite fragile so take extra care to not damage the plants near the lake. Look for good campsites in the forest on the north shore of the lake.

From the saddle between Mud Lake and Gray Lake the Tahoe Rim Trail goes right (southeast) and descends gently 0.25 mile on an open slope above Mud Lake, with additional spectacular views all the way to Fallen Leaf Lake at the far end of Lake Tahoe, in the distance to the south. The TRT then traverses 0.25 mile northeast, exchanging a volcanic trail tread for a granite one. You reach a junction from where the now abandoned Western States Trail descends across private property, and so should be avoided. About 50 feet below this junction, near some willows, is a small spring that can provide water for most of the season. After the snow melts, this is your last source for water until you get to a pond at the intersection of the Tahoe Rim Trail and the Mount Rose Trail about 5 miles away.

With 7.2 miles remaining, start up the TRT on a series of short switchbacks. You soon traverse just below a dramatic large red and black volcanic rock at the top of a ridge. The trail passes just below and to the east of this rock and climbs slightly to the north-facing side of the mountain about 0.75 mile past the junction. Below is Ginny Lake, and in the distance Tahoe Meadows, the Mount Rose Highway, and Mount Rose itself. You now traverse slightly uphill across the north-facing slope to a saddle just below a granite ridge. Here you have crossed a steep slope that will be covered in snow for most of the year. Take care if the pathway is icy. The terrain is spectacular with several large craggy volcanic rocks towering above and a hemlock forest below.

At the saddle, you now face your second 800-foot climb; the first was up to the wilderness boundary below Mt. Baldy. The imposing massif straight ahead would be formidable if you tackled it head-on, but fortunately the TRT does not, and the climb is exceptionally well-graded. From the saddle the TRT has several short switchbacks up among granite boulders, and then it jogs east, then west. Here, it climbs 0.6 mile north and has abundant views, to a switchback just above the east end of a west-trending ridge that climbs to the summit of Relay Peak. Along this ascent, Clark's nutcrackers flit between the scattered gnarled whitebark and western white pines. From the switchback, huge panoramic views open up to the west of Castle Peak, Donner Lake and the Truckee area, and to the south in the distance, Freel Peak above Lake Tahoe. From your vantage point you also have closer views: west down the gaping West Fork Gray Creek Canyon, northwest down equally gaping Gray Creek Canyon, and northeast to a radio-towered peak.

From this switchback, which can lie under snow well into July, you are about halfway up your major ascent. The TRT climbs 0.5 mile southeast up volcanic slopes, and you surpass 10,000' in elevation before you reach a switchback that has poor views. You now have two shorter switchback legs to Relay Peak, the highest point on the entire Tahoe Rim Trail at 10,338' in elevation. On a clear day you can see all the way to Lassen Peak and, rumor has it, Mt. Shasta if the day is crystal clear. The panorama seems unlimited as dozens of narrow valleys and ridgelines unfold before you. Much of what you see in the foreground is the Mount Rose Wilderness. You may see burned trees several ridgetops away providing evidence of the 15,000 acre Martis Fire of June 2001. You also see Mount Rose (10,776') standing out to the northeast in its full volcanic relief. At sunset, the mountain certainly lives up to its name as it takes on a beautiful rosy hue. Finally, to the east-southeast, beyond Tahoe Meadows and Ophir Creek canyon, lies large Washoe Lake.

From Relay Peak your trail now merges with an old abandoned dirt road that heads downhill

Mount Rose from the road next to the radio tower at 10,000' elevation.

and steeply north along the ridgeline to a relay microwave tower developed by AT&T. While the top of the ridgeline provides an excellent location for receiving radio waves, it is unfortunate to see a large ugly tower in this incredibly beautiful location. Near the tower you reach a junction with a broad gravel road, which is still used by vehicles for administrative purposes.

You are now leaving the wilderness, and mountain biking is allowed over the 3.9 miles between here and Highway 431 (Mount Rose Highway). Now you begin a journey down to the Mount Rose Highway. I hope that eventually the Tahoe Rim Trail Association will be able to replace this long journey on a utility road with a trail. With the beautiful terrain in this bowl, a well-developed trail which switchbacks its way up to Relay Peak would be impressive.

On this broad utility road you first descend 0.3 mile south to a switchback, then 0.5 mile northward to a bend east, where you pass an old chair-lift. Before the road to the top of the ridge was built, this chair-lift was constructed as a means to bring the building materials necessary for the relay tower to the top of the mountain; later the lift was used to access the tower during extreme winter periods when snowcats were unable to make the trip to the top. The road descends into a big open bowl with scattered stunted whitebark pine trees. In the winter this area is popular with skiers, snowshoers, and snowmobilers. Now after 1.4 miles of moderately steep downhill on the road, you reach a small pond, known both as Snow Pond (because it is covered in snow much of the year) and as Frog Pond (when not covered in snow, it can be full of frogs).

Sidetrip: Mount Rose

Just above the pond, you meet a junction with the trail to Mount Rose on your left. The 3.4 miles along this spur trail will reward you with the view you get from the top of Rose, which is extraordinary. Along the way wildflowers can be inspiring, especially in summer. Mount Rose is unique in several ways, and has a superb "garden" of alpine plants. One's the woody-fruited evening primrose, which is found only on its slopes. This low-lying plant produces one or more big yellow blossoms on short stalks close to the ground. The flowers, which are pollinated by nocturnal moths, and then die shortly afterward, smell like coconuts. Mount Rose also seems to have its own weather pattern. Often you can hike in shorts and a short sleeve shirt, until the last 0.5 mile, where you encounter fierce winds and chilling temperatures. The top of Mount Rose during a major winter blizzard is truly frightening. The easiest way to the top of Mount Rose is to start at the Tahoe Meadows trailhead, which makes for a 12-mile round trip, with about 2000 feet of climbing, a worthwhile dayhike.

The TRT, from where it meets the Mount Rose trail, follows the road 2.5 miles to the trailhead, on a usually gentle descent, the first half south, the second east. About 1 mile past the pond you get full views of Incline Lake, Lake Tahoe, and Tahoe Meadows. Far below, the next section of the Tahoe Rim Trail can look like a brown snake wandering through the deep green of Tahoe Meadows. The views remain panoramic and inspiring as the road continues gently downhill to the completion of the section at Highway 431, just to the northeast of Tahoe Meadows. The trail ends at a gated entry to the road. To access the next section of the Rim Trail, cross the road and follow it 0.4 mile down to the Tahoe Meadows Trailhead, where you will find a restroom and parking lot.

Tahoe Meadows to Spooner Summit (23.1 miles)

Difficulty—This section is strenuous, mostly due to the length, but also because of elevation gains. While the trail starts at 8740′ and ends at about 7140′, there are two portions of the trail where you encounter climbs of over 700 feet. In the opposite direction, the climb from Spooner Summit to just below Snow Valley Peak is about 1800 feet.

Best Seasons—It is best to hike this section of the trail between mid-June and late October. The segment between Spooner Summit and Snow Valley Peak may be open as early as mid-May in years with light snowfall. However, the section between Twin Lakes and Snow Valley Peak may hold snow well into July.

Highlights—There are spectacular vistas of Lake Tahoe along much of this section of trail. Some of these are the most stunning views to be found anywhere along the Tahoe Rim Trail. In particular, the Christopher's Loop (Herlan Peak) spur trail offers especially remarkable vistas. The trail provides views on both sides of this north-south oriented ridge, of Lake Tahoe to the west, and of the Great Basin to the east. While the thin decomposed granite soils along the trail limit wildflower growth, in several locations flowers can be found in abundance. This is especially the case if you take a side-trip down to Marlette Lake, where the wildflower display is one of the best to be found anywhere. If you are looking for yellow and orange aspen leaves, it is hard to beat the bounty of leaves at Snow Valley, Marlette Lake, and Spooner Lake. Much of this

113

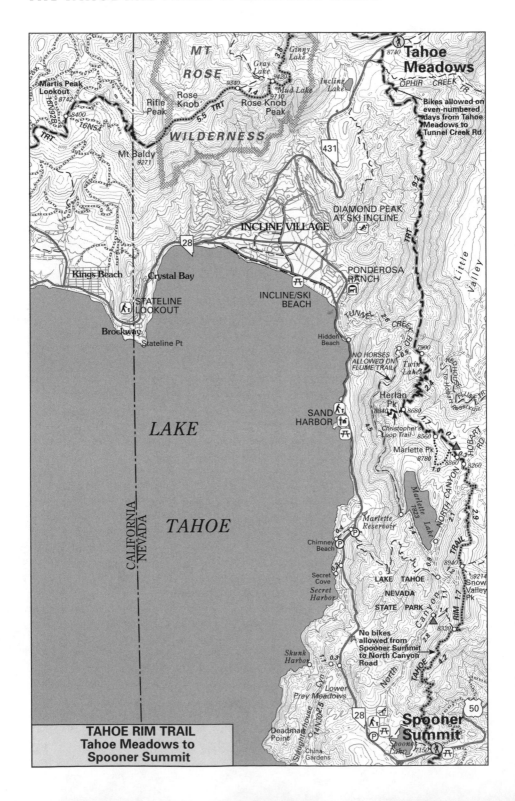

TAHOE RIM TRAIL
Tahoe Meadows to
Spooner Summit

section of trail can be covered on a mountain bike, and, for the experienced rider, affords some of the best mountain biking at Lake Tahoe.

Marlette Lake and Snow Valley Peak.

Heads Up!—Very little water is available on this section of trail. Bring some along for Fido. About 0.7 mile beyond the Tahoe Meadows trailhead, you cross Ophir Creek, a beautiful little stream. At around mile 3 you pass two unreliable seasonal springs. At about 9.5 miles from the trailhead you reach the Twin Lakes. These two small lakes may dry up by late in the summer; as they shrink, the water becomes less attractive, and takes on a green hue. Another source for water is Spooner Lake, near Spooner Summit. If you're "thru-hiking" you should know that there are no trailside sources of water on the next 12 miles south of Spooner Summit. Obtain water at Spooner Lake unless you have made prior arrangements for water to be provided to you. You will see Marlette Lake from the trail. If

115

you are thirsty and/or looking for a swim, it may be a worthwhile detour. From the intersection of the TRT and Hobart Road, it is a 1.75-mile, mostly steep downhill to the lake. About 0.75 mile down, where two gullies converge, there is a usually reliable stream, this may be a good source for water if you are camping at the Marlette Campground, which is about 1 mile from the stream.

Most of the trail is exposed to the sun and wind so bring extra water, extra clothing and lots of sunscreen. Camping is only allowed in two locations: One site, Marlette Peak Campground, is along the TRT near Marlette Peak, about 13 miles south of the Mount Rose trailhead; the second campsite is along North Canyon Road. At a minor saddle, just before you reach Snow Valley Peak take a dirt road 1.2 mile steeply down to North Canyon Road. Turn left and go about 1 mile south down to North Canyon Campground, just east above the road. All you will see is an outhouse, with camping sites behind it out of view from the road. Get water from the stream just to the west of the road. You can also continue on the TRT, past Snow Valley Peak an additional 1.7 miles, to a signed junction with a connector trail, which heads downhill 1.4 miles to the campground.

Tips for Mountain Bikers—For the experienced mountain biker this section of trail is perhaps the best section on the entire Tahoe Rim Trail. It is best to ride from north to south. The Forest Service has ruled that mountain bikers should only use the northernmost 9.2 miles of this section of trail (from Mount Rose Highway to Tunnel Creek Road) on even days of the month so that hikers may experience the trail without bikers on the odd days of the month. After an initial fun ride across the meadow and then along the old Ophir Creek Trail, you turn right and climb to a saddle. Then it is a wonderful, sometimes challenging ride, mostly downhill, for the next 8 miles to Tunnel Creek Road. The trail is sandy and soft in some sections, but in most places it is firm and a real pleasure to ride. Some will feel challenged by portions of the trail; for most, the trouble is well rewarded. At Tunnel Creek Road you can turn right and ride downhill 3 miles to Highway 28 where you can have a shuttle awaiting you. Or you can cross the road and head a short distance to Twin Lakes. The next few miles after Twin Lakes are a challenging steep uphill ride, but well worth the effort since they eventually lead to spectacular views of Marlette Lake and Lake Tahoe. When you reach Hobart Road, turn right. Bikes are not allowed on the rest of this section of the TRT. Hobart Road takes you down to Marlette Lake, where you follow North Canyon Road out to the parking lot at Lake Tahoe Nevada State Park, where fees are required for parking, or for riding through the park.

Getting There, Highway 431 (Mount Rose Highway) to Spooner Summit—The trailhead is located 7.3 miles north on Highway 431 (towards Reno) from the Highway 28 and 431 junction in Incline Village. You will drive past Tahoe Meadows on your right to a parking area and restroom facility on your right. The trail starts from the western edge of the lower parking lot. From Reno, this trailhead is found about 0.75 mile after the highway tops the Mount Rose Summit.

Getting There, Spooner Summit to Highway 431 (Mount Rose Highway)—From Tahoe City you travel 27 miles east on Highway 28 to reach the junction with Highway 50. Turn left on Highway 50 and drive 0.7 mile to the trailhead on the north (left) side of the road (approximately 14 miles northeast of South Lake Tahoe on Highway 50). There is a small dirt parking area on the north side of the highway, situated across from a larger paved parking lot, which provides access to the southbound TRT. It is important to realize that Spooner Summit is not the same as Spooner Lake. Spooner Lake is about 0.5 mile west of the junction of Highways 50 and 28 on Highway 28. Entrance to the popular Spooner Lake area (with access to The Flume Trail) requires a fee, and is reached by driving 0.6 mile northwest from the junction.

Trail Description

From Highway 431, known locally as the Mount Rose Highway, the southbound TRT runs parallel to the highway and descends past several streamlets and then crosses through the middle of Tahoe Meadows, a large subalpine area that can be muddy in June or a wonderful wildflower tromp in July. Stay on the trail to avoid damaging the fragile meadow ecosystem. Near the south edge of the meadow, cross Ophir Creek, a charming year-round stream that is bordered by elephant heads, lupines, and other wildflowers. Except for the fact that you just left the trailhead 0.75 mile back it would be the best source for water on this section of trail. After crossing Ophir Creek, the trail heads into a forest of lodgepole and whitebark pines, and meets the Ophir Creek Trail, where you turn left (south).

For the next 0.2 mile, you are on a smooth, wide trail, walking past lodgepole pines. Soon to the left you see Tahoe Meadows and the radio towers atop Slide Mountain, before the trail meets a junction at 1 mile from the trailhead. (See sidetrip on Ophir Creek Trail, next page.)

The TRT turns right and starts a gentle climb south up the sandy surface past more scattered lodgepole pines, and occasional western white pines and whitebark pines. Exposed to high winds and heavy snows on this north-facing slope, the

Sidetrip: Ophir Creek Trail

Straight ahead is the Ophir Creek Trail which soon heads steeply downhill and eventually reaches Price Lake and in 7 miles, Davis Creek County Park. Along its path there is evidence of the great flood of 1981.

---

trees are smaller than those you will see later on the south-facing side of the ridge. To the north you can see the rose-colored top of Mount Rose.

At 1.7 miles from the trailhead you reach a saddle, about 250 feet above the Ophir Creek Trail. Here you get your first views of Lake Tahoe through the vegetation. The views will just keep getting better and better as the miles go by. Now your pathway is along a long north-south oriented ridge for the next 7.5 miles, going in and out of the tops of east-west oriented gullies. Along the route you will experience numerous gentle ups and downs, and from the saddle will have an overall drop in altitude of about 900 feet to Tunnel Creek Road.

The first mile past the saddle is a gentle, sandy contour along the western slope of the ridge. You pass scattered white granite boulders, appearing as if they were tossed there haphazardly by a giant playing with rocks. Lodgepole pines are now fewer and larger, and some impressively large western white pines are seen with their long narrow cones hanging from the top. Some may mistake the western white pines for sugar pines, but the sugar pine cones are quite a bit larger, and sugar pines are usually found at lower elevations. At 2.5 miles from the trailhead you cross the head of a gully; here the trail changes from its eastern direction to a southern direction. You see a wide view of the lake, looking towards Emerald Bay and Mt. Tallac. Several large, flat granite boulders lie just below the trail making this a great spot to sit and enjoy the views. **119**

Next you ascend gently and enjoy more views of the lake looking towards the Nevada/California border, which lies on a large peninsula jutting straight south into the lake. Soon, about 3 miles from the trailhead, you reach two spring-fed streamlets and colorful lush vegetation which provide a cool break from the dry, sandy terrain that surrounds the area. The trail next winds up and down past a few hemlock trees before reaching another saddle at 3.6 miles from the trailhead with views of Mount Rose to the north. You then begin a short moderately steep descent over a number of evenly spaced granite steps (a joy for the experienced mountain biker), followed by a short climb to another viewpoint.

Every half mile you walk provides an even wider and more beautiful view of the lake. On a clear windy day, the wind ripples shimmer in the sun as the lake turns a deep blue. I have been looking at Lake Tahoe since 1960, and it always seems freshly beautiful. At a little more than 4 miles from the trailhead, your trail now crosses to the east-facing side of the ridge, passing a flat opening with stumps from ancient logging. Here you get your first glimpse of Washoe Lake and the Great Basin to the east. A gentle descent leads to a wider opening with a view of all of Washoe Lake.

At 4.6 miles from your Tahoe Meadows trailhead you go southwest, gently uphill, followed by a moderate descent, back to the west-facing slope. Here where the trail takes a sharp left turn, you find another viewpoint just off the trail to your right. Again, several flat boulders provide a resting spot to appreciate the views. Southwest across Lake Tahoe you see Twin Peaks (8878'), prominent above the northwest shore, and to the southwest, Emerald Bay and behind it, Maggies Peaks (8699' and 8499'). Incline Village lies directly below you to the west.

Past this viewpoint you travel into a thicker forest of red firs and scattered western white pines as you cross to the east-facing side of the ridge once again. Soon, you reach a trail hanging on the edge of the steep bank and pass just to the east of the top of a Diamond Peak Ski Area lift, before reaching a saddle at 5.7 miles from the trailhead. Here you find wide, open, east-facing views toward Carson City and Washoe Lake. The trail next bends to the west and Lake Tahoe so dominates your senses that it appears as if you could walk right into it. Jeffrey pines now predominate, as you head down a short, steep rock staircase (many bikers will want to get off their bikes, others will wish they had half-way down). The long ridge that includes Mt. Baldy, Rose Knob Peak, and Relay Peak can be seen to your north. Below you to the west are the ski runs and condominium developments of Diamond Peak Ski Area, the town of Incline Village, and the Incline area golf courses.

About 1 mile past the Diamond Peak ski lift, the trail climbs through granite boulders to the eastern slope again. Here you pass from the land of Jeffrey pines to the land of red firs, and meander up and down gently through the forest before reaching another viewpoint opening through the trees to the east. About 7 miles from your trailhead, you start a moderate descent on a long switchback. If you are hiking, you will enjoy views to the east of Little Valley and Washoe Lake. If you are on a bike, you will be hanging on, trying not to lose your balance on the deep, soft sand. From the bottom of the descent, you pass ground-hugging pinemat manzanita and chinquapin, before briefly heading through a fir forest, and then back out into a mostly treeless west-facing slope, about 8 miles into your hike.

The final stage of your journey to Tunnel Creek Road is a gentle up and down through a moderately dense forest of red and white firs on a

121

trail cut out of the side of the ridge. Views of the lake are mostly filtered, with one last dramatic viewpoint to the west towards the beaches of Incline Village, Twin Peaks, Dollar Point, and the Lake Forest "island" (a peninsula during low water periods, an island during high water periods). Highway 267 can be seen climbing over the top of Brockway Summit.

At Tunnel Creek Road, 9.2 miles from your trailhead, you meet a junction with the Red House Flume Trail. Now you are in a very busy mountain biking area for much of the year. If you are hiking, keep your eyes open for riders; if you are riding, watch out for hikers.

Sidetrip: Flume Trail

A left turn here soon takes you downhill steeply on the Red House Flume Trail, a popular bike loop in combination with the Flume Trail. A right turn takes you downhill steeply for 0.5 mile to a junction with the Flume Trail. From this junction, a left turn will take you on the Flume Trail (although it is recommended that you ride the Flume Trail the opposite direction, starting from Spooner Lake), a right turn goes down Tunnel Creek Road steeply for 2.6 miles to Highway 28.

To continue on the Tahoe Rim Trail, go straight through level terrain about 0.3 mile to the lower of the two Twin Lakes. These lakes have been the location of several backcountry camps sponsored by mountain biking groups and the Tahoe Rim Trail Association who use the camps as they work to maintain and improve the trail. These shallow grass-lined lakes may dry up by mid-summer after a dry winter.

From the east shore of Lower Twin Lake, you face a 1.5-mile long, 750-foot climb, which usually is moderate, but sometimes is steep, through the

Lake Tahoe from Christopher's Loop.

mixed forest of pine and fir trees. With the soft sand surface, this trail will feel steeper on a bike than if you are hiking. There are occasional views of Mount Rose back to the north and Lake Tahoe to the west. After a series of switchbacks, you almost reach the top of Peak 8706. Traverse west below it, then go south downhill into a level open area, before traversing briefly west and climbing again. This climb is shorter, a mere 0.25 mile, and just before leveling off, you reach a junction at about 2.4 miles from the trail intersection with Tunnel Creek Road. This is the Christopher's Loop spur view trail on Herlan Peak. If you are on your bike leave it here as bikes are not allowed on this viewpoint loop. (See sidetrip, Christopher's Loop Trail, next page.)

You are now about half way through the TRT's Section Three. Heading southeast on the TRT you will find that the route has leveled off before it enters an area that is thick with hemlock trees, which

123

Sidetrip: Christopher's Loop Trail

This 1.2-mile loop trail is well worth the climb. The trail switchbacks steeply up to the top of a sandy ridge. Now you are at the top, but the best viewpoint is still a bit of a walk west toward the lake. Your trail goes across an open plateau and in a fairly short distance reaches Christopher's Loop. You can go either right or left, as both routes will take you to the viewpoint. Once you are there, you are standing on a granite cliff looking down on Sand Harbor while the entire lake unfolds before you. It is the best view of Lake Tahoe I have seen anywhere. The first time you see it, your jaw will drop in amazement. OK, perhaps the second time you see it, your jaw may drop again. The view to the south of Marlette Lake and Snow Valley Peak is also spectacular. This is a great spot to stop for lunch, although at about 12 miles from the trailhead it will take a very early start, or a bike, to get here by lunch time.

can hold the snow until early summer. A short distance farther, you pass through a flat area of scattered pine trees before reaching a wide open treeless ridgetop. Here, about 0.75 mile beyond Christopher's Loop, walk about 100 yards south on a use trail, which ends with inspiring views of most of Marlette Lake in the foreground, and Lake Tahoe in the background. Nearby, Marlette Peak and Snow Valley Peak are visible to the south.

The trail now heads east and down to the eastern slope of the ridge to an area thick with some especially large lupine and paintbrush plants. Stop and gaze to the east for another view over the flowers to the Great Basin. When you continue, you will descend along the east-facing slope past grassy areas with more wildflowers and forested areas of red fir and hemlock. This is a wonderfully enjoyable rolling stretch on a mountain bike. You meet a trail junction at 1.7 miles from the Christopher's Loop junction. From here you have two alternative TRT routes to choose from. The trail to the right is

Sand Harbor from Christopher's Loop.

for hikers only; in 1 mile it traverses the west and south slopes of Marlette Peak, providing panoramic full views of Marlette Lake, Snow Valley Peak, and Lake Tahoe. A left turn at the junction keeps you on the Tahoe Rim Trail, which continues to be multiple use here. You head through more rolling forested terrain and in 0.5 mile, meet the simple Marlette Peak campground with pit toilet and a few picnic tables. No water source is available at the campground. Just 0.2 mile farther it meets the trail which circled Marlette Peak, and the trails are rejoined as one. So which route should you take? If you are bike riding, please only ride on the bike (east) section. If you are a hiker and would enjoy more sensational views take the Marlette Peak Trail, but be aware it is 0.3 mile longer.

From where your trails meet, you head 0.3 mile mostly downhill through open sandy terrain to a

Sidetrip: Marlette Lake

If you need water or would enjoy a swim in a wonderful lake, or, if you are on a mountain bike, leave the Tahoe Rim Trail and turn right on Hobart Road and head 2.1 miles down to a junction by the southeast shore of Marlette Lake. Mountain bikes are not allowed on the remaining portion of this section of the TRT, so you must turn right if you are biking. Hobart Road is level for about 0.5 mile and then heads downhill steeply over some very soft decomposed granite (careful!) to a flatter section of great riding past springtime wildflowers and aspen trees to the junction next to Marlette Lake. The east shore of Marlette Lake in the spring or early summer has one of the most prolific exhibits of wildflowers anywhere. Over 50 different species of flowers are reported to be in this area including lupine, paint-brush, monkshood, horsemint, columbine, tiger lily, and elephant heads. From the junction, a short road descends to the southeast shore of Marlette Lake, where you can stop and swim and then continue south on the main road on your left which heads 0.7 mile to the top of the saddle. Marlette Lake is named after Seneca Hope Marlette, the first Surveyor General of California and one of Tahoe's first mapmakers. From the saddle, follow North Canyon Road the next 3.9 miles of fun hard-packed sand down to the Spooner Lake parking lot. On a bike this is a fun downhill, but watch out for hikers and be sure to obey the speed limits. Yes, speed limits! (5 miles per hour on turns or when passing someone, 20 miles per hour maximum anywhere else). See what happens when an area becomes too popular!

junction with Hobart Road. At this junction, several alternatives are available to you:

At the Hobart Road junction, which is about 14.3 miles from the Tahoe Meadows trailhead, and about 8.8 miles from the Spooner Summit trail-head, the TRT crosses the road and begins the 2.9-mile journey to the saddle below Snow Valley Peak, the ascent with a 700-foot climb. Bikes are not al-lowed between Hobart Road and Spooner Summit on the Tahoe Rim Trail. Head initially east into the trees and soon begin a moderate ascent south. After

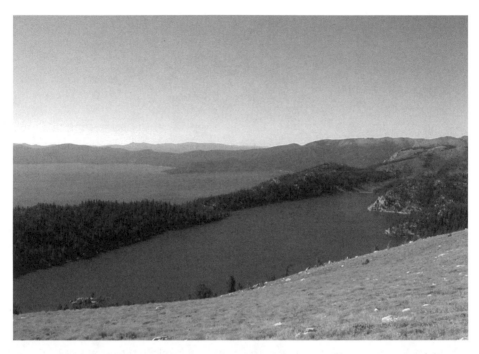

about 0.7 mile, the TRT reaches a jeep road and follows it about 140 yards west before turning south again. If you are low on water, take this road 0.2 mile southwest down a gully to where the road starts a climb northwest. Continue about 200 yards down the gully to a spring. Beyond the jeep road your ascent gets steep as you journey through a forest of red firs and western white pines. You see occasional glimpses of Snow Valley Peak to the south, and of Marlette Lake to your west. As you near the top of the ridge and Snow Valley Peak, there are fewer trees (a few windblown whitebark pines) and the views are more spectacular. You pass through expansive fields of lupine and sagebrush bordered by piles of granite rock boulders. To the north, you can see downtown Reno and its surrounding desert as well as Mount Rose. Just before reaching the saddle below Snow Valley Peak, the trail crosses to the west-facing side of the ridge, providing unobstructed views of Marlette Lake and Lake Tahoe.

Marlette Lake and Lake Tahoe from near Snow Valley Peak.

127

This makes for a wonderful spot for lunch or rest before beginning the long descent to Spooner Summit. At a shallow notch by the northwest base of Snow Valley Peak, the TRT crosses a dirt road coming up from North Canyon below (the large valley and meadow area to the southwest).

Sidetrip: Spooner Lake

To go to Spooner Lake, turn right and in 1.2 miles of steep downhill you will reach a spring and then immediately North Canyon Road where you turn left. From here, an additional 3.8 miles of a moderate, then gentle, downhill path will take you to Spooner Lake at the Lake Tahoe Nevada State Park's parking area. Remember, that is Spooner Lake, not the Spooner Summit trailhead parking lot for the Tahoe Rim Trail. From the junction of the TRT and this dirt road you can also climb in 0.3 mile to the top of Snow Valley Peak, at 9214' the highest peak on the eastern slope of the Tahoe basin. To get there just follow the road east as it climbs up the mountain. The walk to the top of Snow Valley Peak requires an additional 270 feet of climbing for a view that to my mind is not as good as the one of Marlette Lake and Lake Tahoe you just passed. Ah, but peak baggers will have bagged a peak.

If you stay on the Rim Trail heading south, you will hike 5.9 miles from the junction with the dirt road to the trailhead at Spooner Summit. The first mile is a rambling gentle downhill across an exposed ridge with sagebrush, tobacco brush, lots of granite boulders, and a few stunted whitebark pines. You get expansive views of Lake Tahoe, as well as views of the North Canyon Road and a vast forest of aspen trees. The view is especially spectacular in the fall with a sea of yellow aspen leaves. Enjoy the open view because soon you will be in a dense forest. If you have a pair of binoculars, you can count the numerous bikers grunting their way up the steep North Canyon route towards Marlette Lake, and the ever popular Flume Trail.

The Spooner Lake Cross-Country Ski Area operates here in the winter, maintaining groomed trails that head up from Spooner Lake to Marlette Lake, Hobart Road, and depending upon snow conditions, to the top of Snow Valley Peak. In addition, Spooner Lake Outdoor Company owns and operates several very charming log cabins close to the Tahoe Rim Trail that are available for rental year round, as well as a shuttle service for mountain bikers and hikers using the Flume Trail or the Tahoe Rim Trail. For more information contact Spooner Lake Outdoor Company at (775) 749-5349, or at www.theflumetrail.com.

After an abundance of Lake Tahoe views, the trail ventures to the east-facing side of the ridge for views of Eagle Valley, with its sprawling Carson City. Then you head into a thick forest of red fir and Jeffrey pine as the trail continues down the ridge. Along this ridgeline section, as you may have seen earlier on the trail, are old weathered stumps cut as high as 5 to 6 feet off the ground. These trees were cut in the 1870s providing wood for the Marlette Flume below Marlette Lake, from where the wood traveled by water to Carson City, and eventually Virginia City, to support the silver mines. The dry climate of the east shore has kept the trees from further decomposition over all these years. At 1.7 miles from the junction with the trail to the top of Snow Valley Peak, you meet a junction on a minor crest saddle. From here, a trail descends northwest, losing over 700 feet in elevation as it switchbacks in 1.4 miles to the primitive North Canyon Campground and the adjacent North Canyon Road. Near this campground, water can be found at a small creek that flows through a grove of aspens just west of the road.

129

On the TRT, with a little over four miles to go, your trail now winds gently downhill along a heavily forested ridgeline of pine and fir trees. The trail is soft dirt and an easy walk (although if you are doing this whole route in one day, it may not seem easy at this point). Occasional filtered views open up, but this is primarily a walk through a shady forest. At 1.4 miles south of the campground trail junction, a vista trail leads off to the right. After a 100 yard jaunt up this spur trail you will find views of Lake Tahoe and the mountains above the lake's west shore. If you started hiking from the Spooner Summit trailhead, this vista point is 2.8 miles from the trailhead, and 1000 feet above it.

Your gentle-to-moderate walk winds through the forest pathway for another 2.25 miles before ending with a short steep descent to a dirt road. On it the TRT turns left, and you walk 0.5 mile, passing a large grove of aspen trees with filtered views of Spooner Lake, to the end of the section.

Alternative Routes

Do you like the beautiful views, but are not quite ready for a 23-mile jaunt? Take a look at some of these alternative routes that provide for a shorter trip.

- ⋏ Start at the Tahoe Meadows trailhead and hike as far as you want and then turn around. You will find an abundance of great viewpoints and numerous lunch spots on the flat granite rocks. This relatively easy trip makes an excellent route for children.
- ⋏ Start at Tahoe Meadows and hike 9.2 miles south to where the TRT runs into Tunnel Creek Road. Turn right (west) and walk or ride steeply downhill for 3.1 miles to Highway 28. Be careful on the downhill as the sand can be quite deep, especially later in the summer and

fall. If you time it correctly the fall colors
in Tunnel Creek canyon can be spectacular.
Shuttle service may be available through
Spooner Lake Outdoor Company at (775)
749-5349.

⋏ Start at the Spooner North Trailhead and hike
5.9 miles to the saddle below Snow Valley
Peak where you meet a dirt road. Turn left
and follow this road 1.2 miles to where it
intersects the North Canyon Road. Turn left
again and walk 3.8 miles to the Spooner
Lake parking lot. You can then walk around
Spooner Lake and find a trail to the Spooner
Summit parking area.

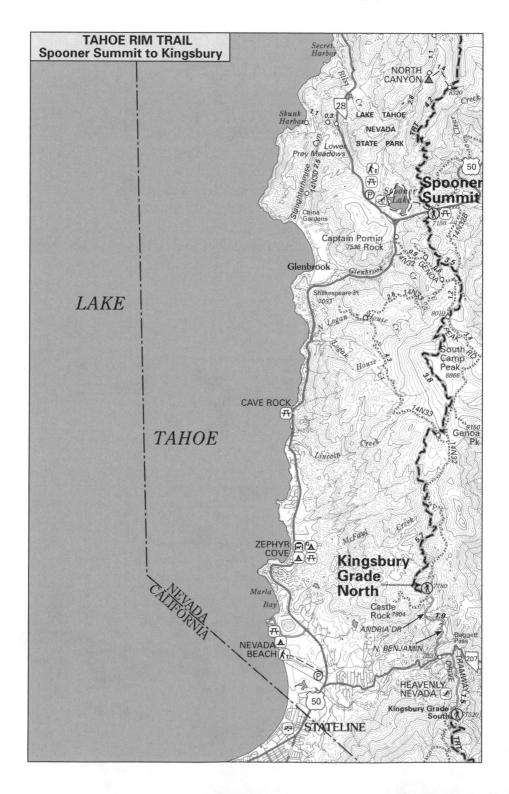

Spooner Summit to Kingsbury Grade (13 miles)

Difficulty—Moderately difficult. There is a steady climb of about 1600 feet in the first five miles, and a wonderful almost level mile in the middle, filled with views. Then the trail is mostly downhill. The starting elevation is 7150', and the ending elevation is 7780', with the high point just a little below the top of South Camp Peak (8866'). This is the easiest section of the Tahoe Rim Trail to hike, particularly in the opposite direction, with just over 1000 feet of elevation gain.

Best Seasons—Early June to late October. As on most of the east shore, the snow melts faster here than on the west shore. There are several heavily forested north-facing sections that may retain snow until late June, but in most areas the snow melts by late May.

Highlights—The biggest highlight of this section is the spectacular view of most of Lake Tahoe, and the west shore, from South Camp Peak. This unobstructed view looks directly up the entrance of Emerald Bay to the mountains of Desolation Wilderness. At South Camp Peak you will find lots of rocks to sit on, and even a wood bench that some kind trail builder provided. This could be the perfect TRT lunch spot, especially since it is about halfway between Spooner Summit and the Kingsbury trailhead. Making South Camp Peak your turn-around point for an out-and-back hike or ride makes good sense whether you are starting from the Spooner Summit trailhead or from Kingsbury Grade.

Heads Up!—Water is not readily available on this

Genoa Peak from South Camp Peak.

section of trail. Be sure to bring plenty of water for yourself and your pets. If you are thru-hiking be sure to fill your water containers at Spooner Lake before you reach the trailhead. While South Camp Peak itself might make a good camping spot, the lack of water makes this hike best for dayhikes. Much of the trail is open and exposed to the sun so be sure to bring plenty of sunscreen. If you are hiking, watch out for mountain bikers, because this is a popular biking trail. If you are biking, watch out for hikers, because it's also popular with hikers. Both groups should watch out for horses.

Tips for Mountain Bikers—Mountain bikes are allowed on this entire section. This ride can be completed from either direction, with the impressive views of South Camp Peak in the middle making a good location for a break. The section from Spooner to South Camp Peak is a great ride. It is an easy-to-moderate climb most of the way on smooth and sandy trails. If you get to the top and turn around, the downhill is a thrill, fun but not too difficult. The section from South Camp Peak to Kingsbury is more technical due to rocky steps and challenging terrain.

Getting There, Spooner Summit to Kingsbury— From the "Y" in Tahoe City drive 27 miles east on Highway 28 past Incline Village to the top of Spooner Summit, where Highway 28 meets Highway 50. Turn left on Highway 50 and drive 0.7 mile to the trailhead parking lot on the right, which has room for 20 cars. Your Spooner-to-Kingsbury trailhead has a pit toilet and several picnic tables in a nice setting under a grove of aspen trees. The trailhead is about 14 miles northeast of South Lake Tahoe on Highway 50. Directly across Highway 50 is the Spooner-to-Highway 431 trailhead.

Getting There, Kingsbury to Spooner Summit— From Highway 50 at Stateline, Nevada drive 2.9 miles up (east) Highway 207 (Kingsbury Grade) and turn left on North Benjamin Drive. (This is 0.3 miles before the top of Daggett Pass). North Benjamin becomes Andria Drive, and you go a total of 1.9 miles from the highway to the end of the pavement and a trailhead with the Tahoe Rim Trail sign on your left.

Trail Description

From Spooner Summit, the mostly sandy trail climbs moderately up a somewhat open slope where manzanita, chinquapin, tobacco brush, and sagebrush grow. In a fairly short time, the grade eases and you begin a steady, but less steep, climb through open forest, meadows, and thicker stands of Jeffrey pines and red firs. Here, the trail is smooth, hard-packed sand, which is wonderful for mountain bikers. This open forest is a popular area for both deer and bear, and at least one mountain lion has been spotted in the area. During the

135

drought period of the early 1990s, a high percentage of trees in the area died because they lacked the necessary moisture to fight off invading bark beetles. In the late 1990s the area was logged heavily to remove the dead trees. The result has been a more open forest and some new dramatic views of the surrounding mountains.

Along the way south toward South Camp Peak, you intermittently glimpse Lake Tahoe and Desolation Wilderness to the west, and Snow Valley Peak to the north. Mule ears, paintbrush, lupine and several aspen groves grow along the trail. After about 550 feet of ascent and 1.5 miles, you reach a little knoll with a short spur trail to the top, providing views into the Carson Valley and to the north toward Snow Valley Peak (9214') and Mount Rose (10,776'), two mountains of the Carson Range. While enjoying the view, contemplate the Carson Range, which is the transition zone between two very different environments. To the west, along the slopes above the western edge of Lake Tahoe, is the heart of the Sierra Nevada, where every winter copious amounts of snow fall. That area is lush with a thick forest, green meadows and countless lakes. The snow lasts well into summer. Where you stand in the Carson Range, on the other hand, receives about half as much snow as the western slope. The trees are more scattered and lakes are rare. The dryer area that you see to the east, begins the basin and range high desert zone, which dominates most of Nevada and Utah. This area receives considerably less annual precipitation than the Carson Range. While many factors determine what the natural surroundings look like, in the western United States the biggest determining factor is how much precipitation an area receives.

About 0.6 mile past the spur trail your route turns from south to east, and after a nearly level

0.4-mile traverse, it crosses a minor road about 250 yards north of where it ends at Genoa Peak Road, a major forest service road. A large aspen grove grows alongside it, but you won't find any flowing water. You've climbed only about 100 feet in the last mile, but now you turn southward and climb gently 0.4 mile to an abandoned road that would take you southeast in 0.25 mile to a pond that usually has water into June. After a second 0.4-mile climb, you reach a second short spur trail, which takes you to less spectacular views. Now you descend 0.3 mile west to a crossing of the major Genoa Peak Road, about 3.5 miles from the trailhead, adjacent to a large open staging area for logging operations. The trail then becomes increasingly steeper as you begin an unrelenting 800 foot climb to the crest of South Camp Peak through heavily forested terrain. You may see signs of logging, including numerous blackened stumps. The trees were cut down and the brush and debris from them was burned. Just before reaching the northwest edge of South Camp Peak, the trail passes through a thickly forested north-facing section where you may see some early summer snow.

South Camp Peak is a large, nearly level, open area with great picnic sites. You walk along the broad summit's west rim; and, its low-lying shrubs do not obstruct the spectacular views, which you have for 1 mile. The summit in fact is so broad and level that "Peak" is certainly a misnomer. The highest rock outcropping is about 0.75 mile along your rim traverse, and looking southeast from it, you see, Genoa Peak, the pointy nearby peak with a radio tower on top. Scanning clockwise, next you see Heavenly Ski Resort and beyond it to the south, the brown, rounded Freel Peak; Stateline, and its casinos, as well as the rest of the South Lake Tahoe area; Fallen Leaf Lake; Desolation Wilderness including the pointy spire of Pyramid Peak, and Mt.

137

Tallac which seems to rise up right from the lake; Emerald Bay, and evidence of the landslide that occurred in 1955, just after the construction of Highway 89 along the bay. Next comes Stony Ridge, with Jacks Peak and the nipple-topped Rubicon Peak; and then to the west, the deep westshore canyons: Blackwood, and Ward (with Twin Peaks on the ridge between the two canyons). Increasingly northwest you see Alpine Meadows, Squaw Valley, and to their north, Castle Peak above Donner Summit. While the views are spectacular, sometimes the winds are ferocious as you gaze from this exposed lookout straight into prevailing westerly winds. From this angle you can see right into Emerald Bay and you may get the mistaken impression that Lake Tahoe is 100 miles long and 5 miles wide. Unless you take a steep sidetrip up to Genoa Peak, this is the highest elevation point along this section of trail, at around 8800′ elevation. If you would like to hike an out-and-back on this section of the TRT, this is the place to turn around. It makes for a wonderful 10- to 12-mile round trip (mileage depending on where you turn around). About midway along the journey across the open area of South Camp Peak, you may discover the small abandoned and caved-in copper mine. This site may be dangerous so avoid exploring.

If you complete the entire point-to-point route from Spooner Summit to Kingsbury Grade, you will probably drag yourself away from the views and start heading gently downhill and away from the sometimes stiff winds in the direction of Genoa Peak. In 0.5 mile you reach a saddle with a dirt road that climbs southeast to Genoa Peak. (See sidetrip to Genoa Peak, next page.)

On the TRT, from the junction with the Genoa Peak jeep road, you begin a 5.7-mile long and usually gentle descent toward Kingsbury Grade. The

Sidetrip: Genoa Peak

In 0.8 mile of steep climbing you will be at the top of Genoa Peak (9150'). The views of Lake Tahoe from the top of Genoa Peak are similar to those from South Camp Peak, but you get the added bonus of views of Carson Valley to the east. On the negative side, you will be standing next to a radio tower. The area around Genoa Peak is popular with glider planes. Once, I saw one fly by so close to the peak that the pilot and I were close enough to wave to each other.

forest here is composed primarily of small young Jeffrey pines, red firs, and western white pines, and you may continue to see the blackened stumps left behind by past logging. About 0.7 mile past the road which led up to Genoa Peak, you cross a small dirt road on the floor of a gully, and here the trail turns northwest and then south as it rounds a peak. You traverse the mountainside on a trail that has become more challenging and technical for mountain bikers. Your path is now bordered by granite boulders and has many rock steps to climb over. The forest has become thicker so you can only get an occasional glimpse of the lake. One of these views, however, is a dramatic look at Emerald Bay and Mt. Tallac, which feels much closer to this section of trail. As you continue on a more narrow, rocky trail, you see Heavenly Ski Resort and its accompanying development. The stark view of high-rise condominiums takes away from the feeling that you are away from it all.

The last mile of the trail rolls up and down along short stretches. Just 0.5 mile shy of the finish, a short vista trail heads off to your right. While the views from the vista point are not nearly as lovely as the views you saw earlier, this vista makes for a pleasant short hike to a viewpoint from the Kingsbury Grade trailhead. Past the viewpoint your trail curves east and soon terminates at the end of a paved road.

   To get to the next section of the TRT you must walk 1.9 miles to Highway 207 on a paved residential road, and then an additional 1.5 miles on the other side of the highway to arrive at the trailhead under the Stagecoach chair-lift at Heavenly Valley. About 0.8 mile north of Highway 207, thru-trekkers can obtain water at George Brautovitch Park, along the road's west side.

Kingsbury Grade to Big Meadow
(23.2 miles)

Difficulty—This long and relatively strenuous section has a lot of elevation changes, and a 9730 foot high point. While a trail of this length is too long for many to hike in one day, for the strong hiker it is a wonderful dayhike.

Best Seasons—Each end of the trail can be hiked as early as mid-June. The highest part of the trail near Freel Peak is usually not open until mid-July or later, depending upon the amount of snow received the previous winter. The first major snows at Freel Peak may come as early as the middle of October.

Highlights—This trail section provides tremendous views of Lake Tahoe, Carson Valley, Desolation Wilderness and the Carson Range. In addition, it has a wonderful high-elevation lake, Star Lake, and access to the summit of the two highest peaks in the Tahoe basin: Freel (10,881') and Jobs Sister (10,823').

Heads Up!—Some sections of the trail are above 9000' in elevation, and much of the trail is open and exposed to the sun and wind—bring your sunscreen. As with all sections of the trail along the east shore of Lake Tahoe, water is in short supply. In the first few miles out from the Stagecoach parking lot, there are several seasonal streams, with the South Fork of Daggett Creek lasting the longest. Star Lake, which you will reach at 8.8 miles from the Kingsbury trailhead, is a beautiful source of water. About 1 mile past Star Lake you find a stream coming down from Freel Peak, a tributary of Cold Creek. On slopes west of Freel Peak, several

141

small streams cascade across the trail into late summer. From Armstrong Pass you may find water by heading southeast from the TRT on the steep Armstrong Pass connector trail. It is 0.4 mile long, and near its bottom you cross a small stream. From its trailhead a dirt road descends almost 0.5 mile to cross larger Willow Creek. You can find reliable water just below the west edge of the western Freel Meadow. Finally, east of the Big Meadow trailhead, there is Grass Lake Creek, at approximately 0.5 mile, and another one at 2 miles from the trailhead at the Grass Lake Trail junction.

Tips for Mountain Bikers—This section is challenging, loved by some and hated by others. It has lots of technical areas with hundreds of rock benches that will require many riders to dismount. Portions of the trail are along steep drops that may unnerve some riders. The first portion is primarily a long steady climb, with the exception of a brief

Freel Peak from high point on the trail (the route to the top of the peak starts here).

143

steep downhill on some very sandy, loose soil. Once you get to the top of Monument Pass, just about when you are wondering why you are doing this, the trail levels off for some great riding for several miles to Star Lake. After Star Lake it is a major, difficult climb again up to 9700'. Almost everyone will be walking his or her bike near the top. From the saddle of Freel Peak, it is time for a big downhill with a few tight little switchbacks that may scare some riders. Eventually, you reach Armstrong Pass, a great place to escape if you have had enough. A short trail descends to a dirt road, Forest Route 051F, that you can follow 0.5 mile down to Forest Route 051 and take it 3.5 miles to Highway 89. If you do this, you will reach Highway 89 0.8 mile east of signed Luther Pass, and 1.8 miles above the Highway 88/89 junction in Hope Valley. If you continue toward Big Meadow, you will confront another long uphill, followed by another long downhill. Along the downhill section, you pass the junction to the Saxon Creek Trail. This very popular mountain biking trail, usually accessed via the Big Meadow trailhead, is known as Mr. Toad's Wild Ride. While some may find it a wild ride, I found it to be very chewed up and steep and impossible to navigate in many sections. If you go, be prepared for difficulty. Past "Mr. Toad's" is a brief steep uphill, followed by a steady downhill to the end of the trail, which is fun, but not without several technically challenging sections.

Getting There, Kingsbury South Trailhead to Big Meadow Trailhead—From Stateline in the South Lake Tahoe area drive east up Highway 207 (Kingsbury Grade) 3.2 miles to Tramway Drive at Daggett Pass, the summit of Kingsbury Grade. Follow the signs 1.5 miles to the Heavenly Valley Resort Stagecoach parking lot. Look for the Tahoe Rim Trail sign at the south end of the parking lot underneath the Stagecoach chairlift.

Getting There, Big Meadow Trailhead to Kingsbury South Trailhead—From the intersection of Highway 89 and Highway 50 in Meyers, drive 5.3 miles south on Highway 89 to the Big Meadow Trailhead and parking area, on your left. Luther Pass is 3.3 miles farther on. This trail can also be accessed from the Grass Lake trailhead, which you will find by driving south on Highway 89 past the Big Meadow trailhead for 1.5 miles. Park on the right side of the road in a roadside pullout and cross the highway to the trail. If you pass Grass Lake, the lake that looks like a meadow on the right, you have gone too far.

Trail Description

Amidst high-rise condominiums and a huge parking lot, the trailhead is located underneath a ski lift. Are we talking a wilderness experience here or what? Don't worry, it gets better. You start with a 0.3-mile, very steep climb to a saddle, where you cross under the Stagecoach ski lift. Up here you go 80 yards south on a road to the trail's resumption, which immediately turns east. The trail switchbacks moderately up through a forest of red firs and Jeffrey pines and provides views of the condos below and later brief glimpses of Lake Tahoe and Washoe Valley. You walk over numerous granite boulders and steps, which are challenging to those on bikes. After climbing for close to 1 mile you reach a saddle and then descend gently for 0.5 mile, passing under another Heavenly Ski Resort ski lift. In another 130 yards you cross the South Fork of Daggett Creek, which runs most of the year. It provides a patch of greenery amongst the thick brown forest. As you ascend again, western white pines and lodgepole pines replace the red firs and

145

Jeffrey pines. Next the trail gently climbs through alternating areas of dense forest and a more open combination of brush and forest with manzanita and tobacco brush dominating the scene. The open vegetation allows views east to Carson Valley and desert ranges beyond it. About 0.75 mile past the creek you reach the north rim of Mott Canyon, where you see Freel Peak. You follow the rim for a 0.5-mile moderate ascent west, then climb gently 0.25 mile south to where, about 3.3 miles from the trailhead, you reach a saddle and a ski area maintenance road. You drop very steeply, but thankfully briefly, on this road over soft sandy soil (careful on your bike!) into Mott Canyon. Just underneath the Mott Canyon chair-lift, is beautiful little Mott Canyon Creek. In the early summer, its banks are covered with

Lewis monkeyflower.

Lewis monkeyflower, yellow monkeyflower, delphinium, and columbine. This stream may dry up by late summer. If you are hiking this section in late summer or fall, the South Fork of Daggett Creek will be your water source between the trailhead and Star Lake.

After a short distance with a moderate climb, you come out of Mott Canyon and round the corner to an open traverse. Your route is now mostly treeless and facing east with stunning views of Carson Valley to the east and Jobs Sister, with its huge drop in elevation from mountain top to valley floor, in the distance to the south. To your left, and steeply below, is evidence of a major forest fire reaching up towards Jobs Sister from the Carson Valley. Here you will see mountain mahogany and the largest western white pine I have ever come upon just to the left side of the trail. With a circumference of 24 feet, the pine provides shade in this hot, exposed section of trail. While beautiful to hike, anyone who is afraid of heights will find this cliff-edge section of trail a challenging bike ride, which becomes steeper toward Monument Pass.

Approximately 5 miles from the trailhead, you climb to Monument Pass, which is crossed by powerlines, and which is about 0.4 mile beyond the Nevada-California boundary. At the pass you cross from the Carson side (eastern slope) to the Tahoe side on the western slope. Monument Peak at over 10,000' is a towering presence to the west. Dramatic views of Jobs Sister and Freel Peak immediately open up.

It is 3.7 miles from Monument Pass to Star Lake. The first two miles are on a gentle, sandy path through mostly open terrain, and provide a wonderful opportunity to marvel at the views of Desolation Wilderness, including Pyramid Peak and the Crystal Range, and Lake Tahoe to the west. As you get closer to Star Lake, the immense size of the Freel Peak massif becomes more and more impressive. A little over 1 mile before Star Lake, the trail begins to ascend again, sometimes steeply, and the tree cover of western white pine, lodgepole, and hemlock gets thicker. Finally you reach Star Lake, located at the base of Jobs Sister, which rises dramatically from its shores. This alluring lake will take your breath away, especially if you venture into its cold waters. As the only large lake on the Tahoe Rim Trail between Mount Rose and Luther Pass, this may be the best place to set up camp for those who are doing an overnight trip. There are several overused camping spots which are too close to the lake to legally camp (remember to camp at least 200 feet away from any body of water), and lots of wonderful camping spots above the lake.

When you leave Star Lake, the trail can be a bit confusing; just follow the rocky pathway over

Star Lake and Jobs Sister.

the lake's outlet. The first mile or so after Star Lake is to me the most interesting mile of this section of the TRT. You begin with a moderate climb from Star Lake, with good views of Lake Tahoe. You are now in the wide open at a high altitude where western white pines, whitebark pines, and hemlocks are scattered amongst the sandy soil. Many of the trees have been tortured by high-altitude winds and are stunted and bent. You also see numerous large pieces of white quartz along this section as well as patches of snow that hang on late into the summer. You head steadily toward 10,000' in elevation, passing an early summer waterfall and then viewing the imposing hulk of Freel Peak. You will arrive at a swiftly moving clear mountain stream, a tributary of Cold Creek. Only a foot or two wide, it creates a green grassy path through the desolate sand and rock. If you head upstream, you will find open terrain, good for camping. As you reach the saddle below Freel Peak, at the high point of 9730', don't be surprised to find a patch of snow even in late July. This often windswept spot is about 1.9 miles south of Star Lake and 3.0 miles north of Armstrong Pass.

Sidetrip: Freel Peak

At this saddle, you can begin a steep climb to the top of Freel Peak, at 10,881' the tallest peak on the Tahoe-basin rim. The path is easy to follow since most trees are gone and it is just a hearty huff and puff along the ridge to the top. (OK, a very hearty huff and puff of about 1150 feet in elevation!) At the top you will find abandoned buildings formerly used by a television station. From Freel Peak you can easily hike cross-country over to the top of Jobs Sister (10,823'). Climbing these peaks makes challenging, but beautiful, jaunts if you are camping in the Star Lake area, and of course the views are spectacular.

Those who find over 23 miles just about enough to hike, can skip Freel Peak and continue on the TRT. Here you are almost midway through Section Five, about 10.7 miles south of the Kingsbury South trailhead, and about 12.5 miles north of the Big Meadow trailhead. Your trail begins with a long steady thinly forested descent 0.7 mile south to a switchback, which turns you back to the north. You continue downhill for an additional 0.3 mile before switching back again to the south. Once again, you will enjoy excellent views of the Crystal Range, the massive granite ridge on the western edge of Desolation Wilderness. You soon cross three spring-fed creeks that are usually flowing and provide much-needed water and beautiful wildflower displays. These little ribbons of color in this dry, brown landscape are a welcome relief. Less than 0.5 mile past the last streamlet is a huge mass of granite with a steep cliff face and lots of fascinating

149

rock formations known as Fountain Face, about 1 mile north of Armstrong Pass.

A Tale of Two Fountains

The Fountain Place you see on the map is a meadow area, below to the west. Both Fountain Face and Fountain Place were named for Garret Fountain, who built a way station at Fountain Place in 1860 in an effort to supply miners on their way from California to the Comstock Lode in Nevada. Fountain hoped they would go over Armstrong Pass, but instead they chose Daggett Pass, and Fountain's dream failed.

Less than 0.3 mile before Armstrong Pass the trail is gently graded; you experience a gentle up and down traverse, and pass many large juniper trees, with their light blue berries and gnarled trunks and branches, along the way.

At the deep crest notch of Armstrong Pass, you can leave the TRT to shorten your hike. (Or, if you come in from Armstrong Pass, it makes for a relatively short way to access Freel Peak.) The short, steep Armstrong Pass trail takes you 0.4 mile to trailhead parking at the end of a dirt road, with access to Highway 89 above Hope Valley in 4 miles. Follow the Armstrong Pass Trailhead directions below in reverse.

The Armstrong Pass junction is located at the top of the "U" shaped valley at the end of the long southward traverse. Here, the trail rounds a corner of the ridge and heads west. From Armstrong Pass, the journey to Big Meadow is 9.5 miles. In just 0.1 mile you reach a junction with a trail that descends northwest toward Fountain Place and Oneidas Street. The TRT quickly leaves the ridge to begin this next phase with a steady, sometimes steep uphill climb on sandy soils through a forest of scattered western white pine, lodgepole pine, and red fir.

Sidetrip: Armstrong Pass

To access Armstrong Pass from Highway 89 (a section of road recommended only for four-wheel drive vehicles with high clearances), take Highway 89, south from the junction of Highway 89 and Highway 50 in Meyers up to signed Luther Pass, just beyond a large grassy meadow holding Grass Lake. Start on a long downhill toward Hope Valley going 0.8 mile to a junction with Forest Service Road 051 on your left. (This junction is 1.8 miles up from the Highway 88 junction down in Hope Valley.) Take this road steeply uphill. In 1.1 miles the road divides. There is a gate on the right fork, but stay left. At 1.6 miles, bear left. At 1.8 miles, you cross a cattle guard, then continue to bear left. At 2.4 miles, you reach your first bridge as you follow a stream. At 2.7 miles, at a fork in the road, go straight ahead. At 3.4 miles, you will reach the second bridge; cross this bridge, then immediately make a 180-degree left turn onto a road numbered Forest Service 051F (this is a good place to park and hike to lessen the chance of damaging your car). Just a little farther at 3.5 miles in from Highway 89, you cross another bridge and the road begins to get quite rough. At 3.7 miles in, turn right. Be careful here as it is easy to believe you should go straight. At 3.9 miles you reach a circular parking area. The Tahoe Rim Trail sign is evident at the end of the parking area. Take this trail 0.4 mile steeply uphill to the junction with the TRT.

Your views are now fewer and less dramatic with occasional glimpses of the Freel massif to your northeast as you switchback up the ridgeline past some large trees. The area between Big Meadow and Armstrong Pass is popular for mountain biking. If you are on your bike, enjoy, but watch out for hikers. Be a little more vigilant if you are hiking. While portions of this section are a fun sandy ride, there are a lot of short rocky sections that will force many riders to get off their bikes; other sections are composed of deep granite gravel that will make it tough whether you are going up or down. After 2 miles of switchbacking uphill, you reach an open, broad ridge with large boulders and with views to the

151

Freel Peak from Monument Pass.

south of numerous peaks above 10,000', including Round Top near Carson Pass at 10,381'.

The trail soon leaves the ridge and proceeds through a rocky area with stone steps, then it continues through an open forest until, at a little less than 3 miles from Armstrong Pass, you traverse the largest of three meadows known as Freel Meadows. USGS maps show this area as Freel Meadows, but are not specific as to how many meadows are included. I found three meadow-like areas within 1.5 miles. The first "meadow" is open slopes dotted with mule ears, lupine, and paintbrush which slopes away from the trail (the actual meadow lies at the base of the slopes). Beautiful Sierra peaks can be seen to the south. Just past the open slopes, you reach an excellent viewpoint to the north. Here you see deep, boggy, Hell Hole Canyon directly below you, and farther in the distance to the north, Lake Tahoe. To the northeast, Freel Peak stands out in full relief. Next, you pass through an open forest before reaching a large grassy meadow to your left (the second meadow). Then shortly you reach a third meadow, this one loaded with wildflowers including corn lily, lupine, and delphinium. You can get water from the west end of this meadow, at the headwaters of Saxon Creek. The Freel Meadows area is a wonderful green divide between the more barren sandy slopes of the higher elevations to the east, and the thick forest that appears after the meadows.

After leaving this meadow, you descend at a moderate pace through denser forest. About 1 mile later, and 5.1 miles from Armstrong Pass, you reach the Saxon Creek Trail (alias "Mr. Toad's Wild Ride") on a broad saddle just above Tucker Flat.

Sidetrip: "Mr. Toad's Wild Ride"

This popular mountain biking trail is usually accessed via the Big Meadow Trailhead, and is known as Mr. Toad's Wild Ride. If you start at Big Meadow, this ride starts with a long uphill followed by a big challenging downhill. Before you ride this section, be sure to read the mountain biking tips at the beginning of this chapter.

With 4.4 miles left, you continue on the TRT over a short uphill section northwest, followed by a short traverse west, then you have 2 miles of meandering downhill through primarily dense forest of red and white firs and western white and Jeffrey pines, until you reach the Grass Lake Trail. Along the way you see several small meadows with many wildflowers, especially mule ears. There are also two viewing spots. The first is near the top on a very short use trail to a rock outcropping with views to the northwest of Lake Tahoe. The second viewpoint is after the trail switchbacks down through the forest to another rock outcropping on the east side of

153

the ridge. Here you have views of the mountains to the east and southeast. A special visual treat is a small creek that you cross, shaded by lush aspen trees that pop out of a jumble of huge granite boulders.

At 2.0 miles from the Big Meadow trailhead, you meet the Grass Lake Trail, an alternative TRT route to Highway 89. On the Grass Lake Trail, you can hike only 0.6 mile to meet Highway 89, which is 1.4 miles less of walking or riding distance (and 400 feet of ascent or descent) than on the trail to the Big Meadows trailhead. If you are heading to the Grass Lake trailhead you will find a moderately steep downhill through the trees to the trailhead located next to Highway 89. You have now had the pleasure of being on the first section of the Tahoe Rim Trail, which was built by the Tahoe Rim Trail Association in 1984.

A reliable stream can be found near the junction of the Grass Lake connector and the Tahoe Rim Trail. There is only one more water source to be found, Grass Lake Creek, in the next 1.6 miles, about 0.4 mile from the end of the trail. If you continue to the Big Meadow trailhead, you will journey through more of the same terrain, a gentle downhill on many switchbacks through a mostly thick forest of predominantly Jeffrey pine and red fir. While Highway 89 cannot be seen from the trail, it often can be heard. At the finish, you will arrive at a paved road, on which you turn left and go 100 yards to the entrance to a large parking lot and restroom facility (no water). The next section of the TRT heads up to Big Meadow, Round Lake and eventually the Pacific Crest Trail and can be found past the restrooms at the southwest corner of the parking lot.

Big Meadow Trailhead to Echo Summit/Echo Lake

(15.3 miles to Echo Summit, 17.5 miles to Echo Lake)

Difficulty—This section is moderately strenuous. Most of the trail is gentle up and down terrain or almost level through meadows or open fields. While there are several sustained climbs, they are not too steep and most will find this section of the TRT not exceptionally difficult. The most difficult portion of the trail is between Bryan Meadow and Benwood Meadow, where you will experience an almost continuous, steep descent (or a steep climb if coming from Echo Summit).

Best Seasons—This section of trail is best hiked from late June to early October. While you may see a few snow patches well into July, the trail is mostly snow-free by late June. The wildflowers come into full bloom in late July or early August, which makes that the best time to hike this section. When those flowers are in bloom you are in for an incredible treat.

Highlights—There are three beautiful lakes on this trip: Round Lake is only a 5.2-mile round trip from the trailhead. Dardanelles is 1.4 miles off the TRT and provides a 6.8-mile round trip. Showers Lake is a good half-way stop at 7 miles into the 15-mile hike (18 miles if you also go to Dardanelles Lake). You will find impressive volcanic rock formations jutting high above the shores of Round Lake, and on the ridges above Meiss Meadows. There are two large meadows, Big Meadow and Meiss Meadows,

which if you come at the right time of year, will provide you with some of the most stunning displays of wildflowers you will see on the Rim Trail. In addition, other interesting flora is found on the trail, including some spectacular juniper trees. At a wonderful large bowl just past Showers Lake, you will encounter waterfalls and numerous wildflower-bordered streams caused by springtime snow melt, and spectacular castle-like volcanic rock formations. This section may have the greatest variety of views and habitats of any section of the TRT.

Heads Up!—While the trail has several good water sources and places to swim, the second half of the trail, between Showers Lake and Echo Summit, has more limited water supplies, especially in the fall. Water can be found at the following locations: About 0.7 mile south of the Big Meadow trailhead in Big Meadow is Big Meadow Creek, which may dry up in the fall. The Upper Truckee River in Meiss

Spectacular bowl west of Showers Lake.

157

Meadows is usually a swift-flowing stream. About half way through the hike is Showers Lake, an excellent water source.

The two miles of the trail descending to Benwood Meadow are quite steep, which can be very hard on the knees and every other body part. From the Echo Summit end, this is a major uphill starting just 1 mile into your hike.

Tips for Mountain Bikers—From the Big Meadow Trailhead bikes are allowed on the first five miles to the junction of the Tahoe Rim Trail and the Pacific Crest Trail. Bikes are not allowed on the Pacific Crest Trail, so this ride is a 10-mile out and back. Much of this ride is technically challenging, with lots of rocks.

Getting There, Big Meadow to Echo Summit— From the intersection of Highway 89 and Highway 50 in Meyers (south of South Lake Tahoe) drive 5.3 miles south on Highway 89 to the Big Meadow Trailhead on your left (this is about 3.3 miles before signed Luther Pass). The previous segment from Kingsbury Grade to Big Meadow trailhead ends here, and you start across the road and head uphill towards Big Meadow. The trailhead has a restroom facility and informational kiosks.

Getting There, Echo Summit to Big Meadow— Drive west on Highway 50 from South Lake Tahoe to the top of Echo Summit (4 miles west of the intersection of Highways 89 and 50 in Meyers). Just 0.3 mile past Echo Summit make a left turn, which is marked with an Echo Summit Sno Park sign. Park on the southern end of the parking lot close to the hill, and begin walking south on the dirt path.

Trail Description

The trail starts out at the lowest point in the Big Meadow Trailhead parking lot (southwest end).

You walk about 250 yards through a forest of white fir, Jeffrey pine, and juniper before you cross High-way 89. Once you cross the road the trail starts south. It is moderately steep, taking you uphill over rocky terrain through a thicker forest of Jeffrey pine, western white pine, and fir. After a little more than 0.2 mile you pass to the left of Big Meadow Creek, its bed filled with huge granite boulders and lined with aspen trees. By 0.3 mile from the trail-head the grade moderates, becoming almost level as you walk close to a stream on the right sur-rounded in the fall by the yellow leaves of aspen trees. Stop and shut your eyes and listen to the quaking sound that gives the aspen its name. Soon you reach a junction. A left turn here would take you to Scotts Lake. Your trail, however, continues straight ahead to a large flat meadow with the new and original name of "Big Meadow." Just as you enter the meadow, the trail crosses a stream, which is good sized in the spring, but may dry up in late summer. This is, of course, Big Meadow Creek. As you head south across the meadow you are treated to views of the surrounding mountains to your southwest. At only 0.7 mile from the trailhead, you can reach the meadow in half an hour and enjoy a wonderful setting.

After you cross the meadow, the trail heads up-hill again through the fairly dense forest of lodge-pole, western white pine, and red fir. The tree cover thins out as you reach more open and sunny areas with sagebrush and a variety of wildflowers includ-ing lupine, mule ears, and pennyroyal. You now oc-casionally pass small groves of aspen trees. About 1 mile past the meadow you reach a saddle, pass through a barbed-wire fence and head 0.25 mile downhill on a steep section of trail that affords you great mountain views to the south and west. At 2 miles from the trailhead you reach a junction. To your right, the Meiss Meadows Trail (Christmas

Former cowboy cabins in Meiss Meadows.

Valley on the sign) will take you toward Dardanelles Lake in 1.4 miles. (See sidetrip to Dardanelles Lake, next page.)

On the TRT you continue straight ahead and begin to roller coaster up and down through some very interesting volcanic rock mudflow formations. At 2.6 miles from the trailhead (and 0.6 mile from the last junction), you reach the northeast corner of Round Lake. Round Lake is the largest lake you will encounter on this section of trail, and makes for great swimming and camping. The best campsite is at the lake's northwest corner by the outlet, but the lake can get crowded on a sunny summer weekend. Thanks to an influx of volcanic sediments, Round Lake's color varies from a brownish-green to an unusual aqua-blue, more reminiscent of the lakes and streams of western Canada than most of the lakes in the Sierra. As you walk past Round Lake, a spectacular steep cliff of volcanic rock reaches skyward

Sidetrip: Dardanelles Lake

To reach Dardanelles Lake, you descend northwest on the Meiss Meadows Trail for 0.2 miles through a mixed forest of pine, fir, and a few junipers, to another trail which you take; you will hike an additional 1.2 miles on it to Dardanelles Lake. The trail first crosses a creek, then levels off in a grassy meadow before it climbs again up a rocky tread. You reach Dardanelles Lake on a big granite flat that overlooks the lake. Above the lake's south shore is a massive rock cliff reaching right down to the water. There are great camping spots at Dardanelles Lake above a large flat expanse of granite that reaches down to the northeast shore of the lake. The midsummer water can be warm in this beautiful lake so enjoy a swim and then bask on the granite slab. Ah . . . now you know why you put that backpack on. Be forewarned, however, at only 3.4 miles from the trailhead you are not likely to be swimming alone.

on your left. Known as the Dardanelles, you will have the pleasure of gazing at this fascinating rock formation from several locations as you complete your hike.

Just past Round Lake you pass a small seasonal stream and lush meadow area with willows and wildflowers, including lupine, monkshood, Lewis monkeyflower, paintbrush, ranger's buttons and groundsel. You then ascend to an open area with aspen, sagebrush, and grasses that provides views of the volcanic ridgeline to your west. The next 0.5 mile or so is a pleasant, mostly level walk through wildflowers and scattered aspen groves quaking in the wind. Beautiful mountain views are available in every direction. You then begin a gentle ascent into a forest of scattered conifers, then downhill again past a luscious meadow with more mountain views before you reach the Pacific Crest Trail at 4.9 miles in from your trailhead. Across the large open meadow, you will see a charming old cowboy cabin.

Dardanelles Lake, and its high cliffs.

You have now reached the Pacific Crest Trail (PCT), which travels from Canada to Mexico. If Mexico is your goal, turn left, and in a few months you will be there on the PCT. If you would prefer heading up to Canada, turn right. Either way, it's a long trip. This junction is located at the southernmost point of the Tahoe Rim Trail, and as you turn right at the junction you begin heading north. For about the next 50 miles the PCT and TRT are one trail. In addition to the Pacific Crest Trail and the Tahoe Rim Trail, your footpath is now also a part of the Tahoe-Yosemite Trail (TYT), which travels from Tuolumne Meadows in Yosemite to Meeks Bay on the west shore of Lake Tahoe, a distance of a little over 185 miles. The PCT/TRT and TYT are one trail for the next 29 miles, until the TYT heads over Phipps Pass, past a chain of lakes known as the Tallant Lakes, down to Meeks Bay.

You turn right at this junction and begin your journey northwest with a lovely walk up the long valley of the Upper Truckee River. With high volcanic ridges to the east and west, and a beautiful almost-level valley floor to walk across, seasonally filled with wildflowers, it can be a highlight of your day. The flowers will vary from year to year, but you can expect to see low lying lupine and elephant heads in prolific display. As you walk northwest for about 0.5 mile on the PCT, Meiss Lake can be seen across 0.5 mile of swampy meadow to the north. This very shallow, warm lake makes a pleasant swimming hole in late summer. During the early summer, the walk to the lake is swampy, and you may lose blood to mosquitoes.

Mostly through the meadow you meet the Upper Truckee River, a good source for water or for catching your breath, but a potentially wet ford in early summer. After 1.5 miles through the meadow, a fairly steep climb awaits you for the last 0.5 mile up to Showers Lake. This steady uphill push through a mixture of deep forest and open fields gives you prolific displays of tall lupine and paintbrush. As you rise, you will be rewarded with glorious views to the south and east of Meiss Meadows and the Dardanelles.

Showers Lake itself is beautiful (although often crowded with campers). The south side is marshy but the northern side provides great swimming opportunities enhanced by flat granite rocks that reach down to the water. Several camping spots surrounded by hemlock, lodgepole pines, and before late summer, mosquitoes, can be found above the north and east sides of the lake. To continue past Showers Lake, your trail first heads steeply down below the lake's outlet, and then climbs back up on the other side of the outlet's gully. You head for the next 0.5 mile through a pleasant forest with

163

Lupine.

scattered trees and a few wildflower-dotted meadows until reaching the edge of an enormous bowl. This 0.7-mile-wide bowl is a beautiful mixture of castle-shaped volcanic rock formations, little streams plunging down steep rocky gullies, thick fields of lupine and paintbrush, and sometimes even late season snowfields. Several swiftly moving cascades, and stunning views to the east of Lake Tahoe, Dardanelles Lake, and Freel Peak complete this idyllic picture. It is a gentle climb across the bowl and during mid-summer the streams cascading down from the slopes above provide water for you and support an abundance of wildflowers. Near the end of the bowl, the path becomes steeper and the terrain, drier, until you reach a minor saddle on a crest where the surroundings change. Now you enter an area with sandy soils and scattered trees; mostly western white pine, lodgepole pine and hemlock. First you climb slowly, and then the trail levels off and soon reaches the Schneider Cow Camp Trail, which turns to your left and heads first west and then southwest. Now at 1.9 miles north of Showers Lake you continue north and make a 0.2-mile moderate descent to a saddle with an un-marked trail. Past this saddle junction your broad-crest trail continues through the open hemlock forest, making several minor ascents and descents before leveling off and passing several more small meadows. At 3.5 miles from Showers Lake (and 1.6 miles north of the Schneider Cow Camp trail junction), you meet another saddle junction, where a faded marked trail leads to Sayles Canyon. The Trail appears to be in danger of disappearing altogether.

The TRT continues along the sandy crest, mostly devoid of views, until a nice view opens up to the northwest, of Pyramid Peak, the tallest peak of the huge granite ridgeline known as the Crystal Range, which lies in the heart of Desolation Wilder-ness. Tahoe Rim Trail thru-hikers will get much closer views of the Crystal Range as they walk along Lake Aloha about 15 miles north of here, but first you must finish this section. At 4.4 miles from Showers Lake, you reach Bryan Meadow, and the Bryan Meadow Trail, which is about 3.9 miles from the Echo Summit trailhead. (See sidetrip on the Sayles Canyon Trail, next page.)

On the TRT just past the meadow you first de-scend briefly east to a minor gully, then climb, sometimes steeply, through a thick forest almost 0.5 mile to a ridge. After a steep uphill, what do you do next? Go downhill steeply of course, passing a rock outcropping just off the trail to the right. From here views can be enjoyed of the Upper Truckee River Canyon, South Lake Tahoe Airport and Lake Tahoe in the distance. Your trail quickly levels off and you pass a pleasant little camping spot next to a small,

Sidetrip: Sayles Canyon Trail

The Bryan Meadows Trail will join the Sayles Canyon Trail, and as one, it descends an additional 0.6 miles to reach trailhead parking near the Sierra at a Tahoe ski area. These trails provide another means to access Showers Lake for those in the Upper Highway 50 area. Bryan Meadow is a large, gently sloping meadow of grass and seasonal mud, but with no apparent drinking water near the trail. However, you should find water about 0.5 mile down the Sayles Canyon trail, at or just below the west end of the meadow.

usually reliable, stream in a flat area in the trees. This is one of the last good spots to camp before you reach Echo Summit.

Beyond it you begin a descent that starts out steep, and becomes really steep as the trail heads down along the side of a granite ridge. The last time I walked this trail I described this downhill as bone-jarring, toe-jamming, and knee-breaking. And those are just the words I can repeat. The rocky descent is so steep at times, it becomes slippery, so watch your step. The trail follows the east ridge of a big granite canyon that ends at Benwood Meadow. Take a few foot breaks to enjoy the beautiful granite rock formations and the especially large hemlocks you pass. Keep your eyes open for marmots as this is their prime territory. Gazing across this deep canyon, you see a higher ridge of granite on the west side. You pass a massive juniper at a crest saddle, which provides a viewpoint to the south. Views are highlighted by the Dardanelles and Round Top peak, which holds its north-facing snow fields well into late summer. Eventually the downhill largely abates, after a grueling 2-mile descent, where you cross the canyon's stream on a wooden bridge, and head into a lush shady area loaded with tiger lilies, thimbleberries, and ferns. Over the next 0.75 mile

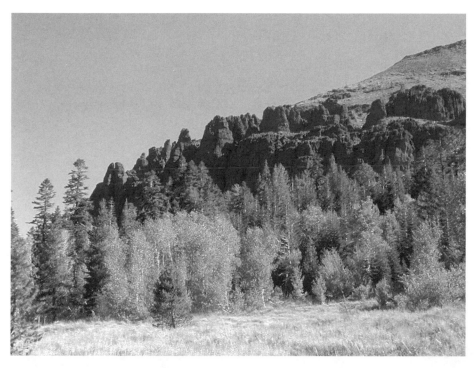

Aspens and the Dardanelles volcanic formation.

you continue on a gentle downhill, with Benwood Meadow visible through the trees on your right. By the meadow's northeast edge, you reach a junction with an older trail coming from a little-used alternate trailhead. With only 0.75 mile remaining, turn left at the junction and ascend gently north through a more open, drier forest of large Jeffrey pines and manzanita. A short distance before reaching the parking area you cross an old dirt road on a mostly treeless slope, formerly a ski area, and head past the headquarters of the California Conservation Corps on your right to a large parking lot. Walk 0.25 mile across the parking lot to Highway 50 and the next stretch of the Tahoe Rim Trail.

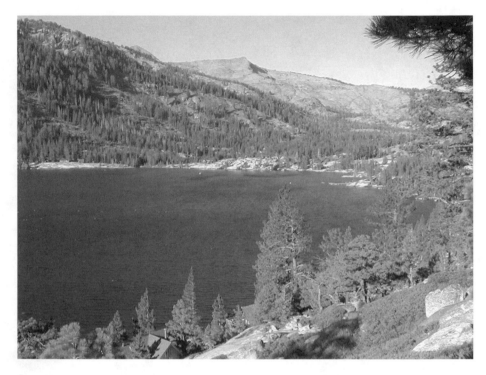

*Lower
Echo Lake.*

Echo Summit/Echo Lake to
Barker Pass (32.5 miles from Echo Lake,
34.7 miles from Echo Summit)

Difficulty—This strenuous section has many ascents and descents. While other segments of the
Rim Trail can be hiked or biked in a day, this trip
for most requires at least two days, and I recommend three. It can also be completed in sections by
hiking out to Fallen Leaf Lake on the Glen Alpine
trail, or to Emerald Bay from either Dicks Lake or
Middle Velma Lake via the Bay View Trail.

Best Seasons—In the typical year, most of this section is snow free from mid-July to late October. Sections of this trail, especially the area on the north
side of Dicks Pass, may have patches of snow into
August following heavy snow years.

Highlights—A wonderful wilderness experience
awaits you as you travel through the heart of Desolation Wilderness. There are many beautiful lakes,
that you will pass by or see from the trail, including
Lower Echo, Upper Echo, Cagwin, Ralston, Tamarack, Aloha, Heather, Susie, Grass, Gilmore, Half
Moon, Alta Morris, Dicks, Fontanillis, Upper Velma,
Middle Velma, and Richardson. If you like to swim
in mountain lakes, this is the trail for you. You will
also cross a high mountain pass with incredible
views into two enormous watersheds.

Heads Up!—The starting elevation is about 7400'
at Echo Lake, and you will rise to nearly 9400' at
Dicks Pass. Water is plentiful for most of the trail,
until you get north of Middle Velma Lake where the
water supplies can quickly decline between it and

169

TAHOE RIM TRAIL
Echo Lake to Barker Pass-Map 1

TAHOE RIM TRAIL
Echo Lake to Barker Pass-Map 2

Richardson Lake. Beyond the latter, there are several streams and springs. The biggest year-round stream along this stretch is Miller Creek, located about 1.75 miles north of Richardson Lake. If you are thru-hiking, consider that north of Barker Pass it is another 2 miles before you reach water again.

Wilderness permits are required to enter Desolation Wilderness. Day-use permits are available at the trailhead. If you are camping you must obtain a permit through the Forest Service. (Permit information can be found in Chapter 1.) The biggest concern with this section of trail, however, is that it is so magnificent that you may want to stay forever, so be sure to bring along enough food.

Getting There, Echo to Barker—This trail begins at either Echo Summit or Lower Echo Lake. Most people prefer to start at Lower Echo Lake, where you can avoid 2.2 miles of mostly viewless hiking, much of it close to Highway 50 or amongst summer cabins.

Getting There, Echo Summit to Lower Echo Lake—From Meyers take Highway 50 westbound to Echo Summit. From the summit, drive just 0.3 miles and turn left. You will see an Echo Summit Sno-Park sign and then a California Conservation Corps sign. Park in the large parking lot and then walk to the western edge of the lot where you will see a Pacific Crest Trail/Tahoe Rim Trail sign marker. The trail parallels Highway 50 west through a mostly level to gently downhill, lightly forested area with some large red fir, western white pine, and lodgepole pine. You meet a dirt road 0.7 mile from the start; cross the road and turn right, then cross above a creek to adjacent Highway 50. Cross this very busy highway to where the trail resumes on the other side. Now the trail heads gently uphill through a thicker forest for 0.2 mile to Johnson Pass Road, the access road that you would take if you were starting at Echo Lake. You cross the road and head up a steep embankment and see a swift moving stream to the left. With 1.1 miles to go to Lower Echo Lake, the trail crosses the stream, which could be challenging when filled with mid-summer snowmelt. Walk through a lush and moist forest that will hold the snow until mid-summer, and then provide late summer wildflowers. Soon after, you pass several summer cabins and head downhill to the Lower Echo Lake's parking area. Cross this large paved parking lot, and another smaller dirt parking lot, to a short trail. You will find restroom facilities and the Echo Chalet Store here before you cross the lake's dam and reach the main trailhead.

Getting There, from Lower Echo Lake—From South Lake Tahoe drive west on Highway 50 to Echo Summit. From Echo Summit, drive 1 mile and turn right on Johnson Pass Road. Take this road 0.6 mile to a junction, where you will turn left on Echo Lakes Road. Go an additional 0.9 mile to a large parking lot above the lake. The resort requests that people using the trail not park in the lower parking lot near the lake. You reach the trail by walking from the Echo Chalet Store, and the lower parking lot, over the dam to a Tahoe Rim Trail sign. This section of the Tahoe Rim Trail is also part of the Tahoe-Yosemite Trail and the Pacific Crest Trail. It is one of the more popular trails into Desolation Wilderness.

Getting There, Barker Pass to Echo Lake/Summit—Take Highway 89 (West Lake Blvd.) about 4.25 miles south from Tahoe City and turn right onto Blackwood Canyon Road, starting opposite Kaspian Beach. Drive 7 miles to the crest above Blackwood Canyon to where the paved road turns to dirt, then another 0.2 mile to the Pacific Crest Trail trailhead dirt parking lot on your right. To ac-

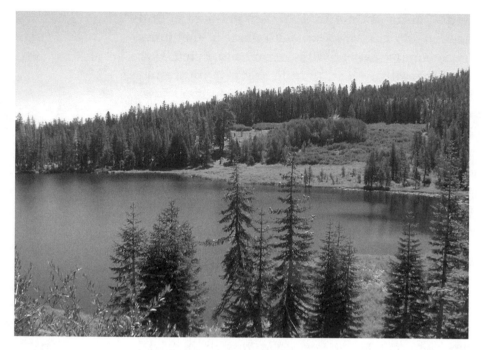

Richardson Lake.

cess the trail, walk south across the dirt road and walk uphill about 50 yards.

Trail Description

From Lower Echo Lake's dam, the trail heads initially east and uphill, and near a switchback west you can have a view toward South Lake Tahoe and Meyers. You walk west above the northern shore of the long narrow Lower Echo Lake. Your route is mostly minor ups and downs, bordered by spectacular granite formations and the deep blue lake and surrounding mountains. The most dramatic granite cliff towering above you to the north is topped with a flagpole, which explains why its name is Flagpole Peak (8363'). The trail rambles for about 1 mile and passes a few gnarled junipers and Jeffrey pines that are hanging on through cracks in the granite. Then it ascends above lakeshore cabins. Your footing becomes more challenging as the terrain becomes rockier. You pass the west end of Lower Echo Lake. Magnificent views of the entire lake open up and you will see some more charming rustic cabins along its granite shore. If you yell at Echo Lakes on a nice calm day, you are supposed to get an echo back.

After a traverse, you then curve south over the rocky peninsula between Lower and Upper Echo Lakes. At 2.5 miles you come to a junction. A left turn takes you on a short trail down to a pier, which provides access to Upper Echo Lake and the Echo Lakes Water Taxi. The resort provides this fee service for homeowners who reside along the lakes, and for hikers heading into Desolation Wilderness. The water taxi, which travels from the Echo Chalet and marina at the east end of Lower Echo Lake to Upper Echo Lake, cuts off 2.5 miles from your hiking distances (5 miles round trip). For information on the Water Taxi call the Echo Chalet at (530) 659-7207. The taxi pier is also a great location for an afternoon swim.

Continue on the TRT from the junction, and climb steadily on more rocky terrain. You can enjoy breathtaking views of both Upper and Lower Echo lakes from this section of trail. Upper Echo Lake is especially striking with its multiple granite islands topped with windblown trees. At 0.6 mile from the boat taxi your trail levels off briefly and you arrive at the boundary of Desolation Wilderness. To hike beyond this point requires a permit, which should be obtained at the trailhead or through the Forest Service (permit information can be found in Chapter 1). You will be hiking in Desolation Wilderness for more than 20 miles on the Tahoe Rim Trail. Just past the wilderness boundary you reach a junction. To your right, there is a trail that leads steeply uphill to Triangle Lake, with access to Echo Peak (8895') (see Sidetrip to Triangle Lake below). You continue on the TRT/PCT, however, climbing 0.5

175

mile to a junction on your left that leads to nearby Tamarack Lake. The trail to this charming lake is located 3.6 miles from the Echo Lakes Trailhead (and just 1.1 miles from the taxi), just inside the wilderness boundary. While it is a great place to stop, it is too close to the trailhead to recommend for camping. Your views are glorious with the im-

Sidetrip: Triangle Lake

This side trail leads to Triangle Lake, then over a steep ridge down to just east of Lily Lake and then by road down to Fallen Leaf Lake. The steep downhill trip is pretty with many lush stream crossings loaded with early summer wildflowers. The trail faces north, however, with snow lasting well into the summer. If you hike this section before July you may find several dangerous icy spots.

posing Ralston Peak (9235') to the south, and Echo Peak to the northeast.

After another 0.7 mile of rocky climbing, you reach another junction on your right.

The climb west finally abates in 0.4 mile at a junction in Haypress Meadows. Here you encounter a mixed forest of red firs, mountain hemlocks, and western white pines scattered around small grassy meadows that bloom with wildflowers throughout the spring and summer seasons. The trail southwest heads over to Lake of the Woods, as does a southbound one 300 yards later. About 150 yards past it you meet a trail descending north to lovely Lake Lucille and Lake Margery. About 0.3 mile later, at 5.2 miles from your trailhead, you meet another junction. The left turn takes you 0.5 mile west down to the southeast corner of Lake Aloha (from where one can wind 0.75 mile west over to the lake's 20-foot-high dam). The TRT and PCT go straight ahead, through an area thick with midsummer wildflowers, to the east shore of Lake Aloha in 0.8 mile. This heavily forested trail section may be covered in snow through early summer.

Lake Aloha with its beautiful plant and rock formations.

Lake Aloha (8116′) provides an incredible, unique landscape. There are only a few wind beaten trees surrounding the lake, with hundreds of small flat rock islands scattered across its surface. The Crystal Range, a huge ridge of granite, topped by pointy Pyramid Peak (9983′) in the south, and Mt. Price (9976′) in the north, rises right up from the western shores of the lake. The trail meanders between granite boulders hugging the shore of Lake Aloha. Above the lake to the east is Cracked Crag, a big pile of rocks that families of marmots call home. Along the entire length of the barren landscape above Lake Aloha, you will find great swimming and camping spots. A dam controls the waters of Lake Aloha and the lake's size decreases

Heather Lake with Pyramid Peak and the Crystal Range in the background.

dramatically in the fall. That great waterside spot you visited in July may be a long distance from the shore after Labor Day.

When you reach the northeast corner of the lake, you meet a junction, 1.4 miles from the last. Straight ahead a trail goes over Mosquito Pass (sounds enticing doesn't it?). The TRT turns right, following the sign, which says Glen Alpine. With Freel Peak (10,881') visible in the distance the trail begins a descent, that in 0.5 mile will bring you to the north shore of Heather Lake. Along the way, you will pass stunning multi-colored rocky panoramas, lots of flowing water, early summer wildflowers, hemlock, and mountain heather topped with its small red flowers. In the early summer much of this area may be under snow. Heather Lake is a picturesque large mountain lake with several tree-topped islands. A limited supply of campsites can be found above the lake. Your 0.3-mile traverse along the north side of the lake towards its outlet provides a special photo opportunity looking west: Heather Lake's biggest island is in the foreground, and the Crystal Range looms above the lake in the background.

Just past Heather Lake, a very unique phenomenon is often visible in spring or early summer. Where the outlet creek melts under the snow, it forms a snow tunnel. I have seen it where the entrance to the snowcave was 10 feet high and at least 30 feet deep. Stepping into the cave will provide you with a shower as well as the sight of the sun filtering through the blue geodesic shapes of the suncups above.

You now walk over a low, rocky saddle and begin a short descent to Susie Lake, another beautiful Sierra lake, and this one bordered by red rock and dotted with islands. Susie Lake is loaded with campsites near its shore, many of which are illegal. Camps are required to be at least 200 feet from the shores of any lake, and you may be cited if you camp any nearer to the water. Unfortunately, Susie Lake can be quite busy due to its short distance of about 4 miles from the popular Glen Alpine trailhead above Fallen Leaf Lake. The trail circles about half of the lake and offers views of the very imposing Dicks Peak (9974') to the northwest, Jacks Peak (9856') to the west and the saddle of Dicks Pass (north) 1600 feet above you. This awesome view may lose some of its appeal when you realize that Dicks Pass is your next major goal. Perhaps you should stop at Susie Lake for a swim and relax before making the big jaunt up the hill. About halfway along your trip around the lake, just before you reach the outlet for Susie Lake, about 1 mile past Heather Lake's outlet and a little over 9 miles from your trailhead, go around the bend to the right and traverse along the side of the hill about

179

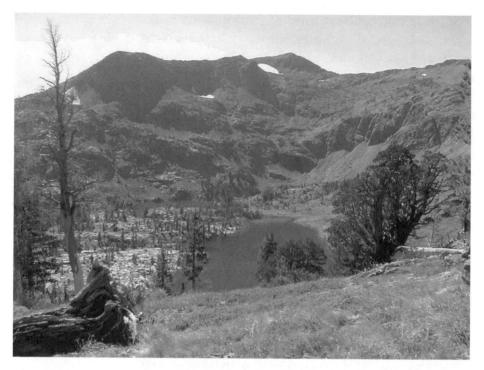

Jacks Peak and Half Moon Lake from Dicks Pass.

50 yards to a tremendous viewpoint of Grass Lake and Keiths Dome to the southeast. Then, return to the trail and cross the outlet creek. In the spring this crossing can be quite a challenge. Try going slightly upstream and cross on the logs. Be careful. Across the creek, hopefully still dry, continue around Susie Lake on the rocky terrain. After 0.25 mile, the trail veers east away from the lake and heads downhill (yes downhill, all of which and more must be made up a little farther on). In about 0.5 mile you reach a junction. A right turn heads 3.8 miles to the Glen Alpine trailhead above Fallen Leaf Lake. You, however will continue straight ahead on the TRT. After a short distance of 0.4 mile, you meet another junction that will take you to Half Moon Lake. (See sidetrip to Half Moon Lake, next page.)

A right leads you to Fallen Leaf Lake in 3.6 miles. From here, the TRT begins a climb of 3.5 miles to Dicks Pass at 9380'. After a steady uphill

Sidetrip: Half Moon Lake

Turning left at the junction just beyond the Glen Alpine trailhead junction, you will be headed toward Half Moon Lake, which you will reach in just 1.2 miles. Alta Morris Lake is an additional 0.7 mile. These lakes are both worthwhile goals for another trip. They lie at the foot of Dicks Peak and Jacks Peak, at the edge of a massive cirque. They may be less crowded than lakes along the TRT/PCT.

Sidetrip: Gilmore Lake

To visit Gilmore Lake, you can go an additional 0.2 mile straight ahead from the Dicks Pass/Gilmore Lake junction. Gilmore Lake is a large round lake bordered by big red firs and lodgepole pines that makes a pleasant spot for a visit, or an overnight stay, especially if you want to hike up nearby Mt. Tallac (9735'), which is about 1.75 miles farther and about 1450 feet higher. Tallac's panoramic views of Lake Tahoe are considered among the best. At just under 11 miles from the Echo Lake trailhead, this may make an excellent camping choice.

grind, you reach a junction at 0.6 mile from the Half Moon Lake trail junction. (See sidetrip to Gilmore Lake, above.)

Ahead the TRT is well graded. Starting gently, it then becomes a more moderate climb toward a conspicuous saddle. Along the way, the views of Susie Lake, Half Moon Lake and Alta Morris Lake are magnificent. In the summer, and sometimes as late as early fall, wildflowers grow in abundance here, especially paintbrush and lupine, which may be seen in huge fields of flowers. In the fall you may also see an occasional explorer's gentian. While much of the journey is treeless, you will pass several gnarled junipers, which have been battered by the wind, as well as some hemlocks and western white

Explorer's gentian.

pines. The trail reaches the saddle between Dicks Pass and Dicks Peak at 9974' elevation. From this location, your north view includes all of Dicks Lake directly below, as well as Fontanillis Lake, Middle Velma Lake, and a wide panorama of mountains in the distance including Twin Peaks (8878') about 20 miles away, and on a clear day, Lassen Peak (10,457') at over 130 miles away. Since the trail is covered in snow much of the year, it is important to understand the distinction between the saddle and the pass. While from the saddle it is another 200 feet of climbing to the pass, don't try to avoid the climb by starting towards Dicks Lake from the saddle. It is a very steep north-facing slope that is covered in ice for much of the year. To reach the pass, continue on the trail east past a few particularly twisted whitebark pines to a level, treeless pass at 9380'. You have now climbed 1100 feet over 2.9 miles, since the junction near Gilmore Lake. Once you reach the top of the pass, you may be ready to collapse, I mean relax, and enjoy the view. And what a view! To the south, you can see Lake Aloha, Pyramid Peak and the tip of Mt. Price, Susie Lake, Half Moon Lake, Alta Morris Lake, and all the way south-southeast to Round Top (10,381′) about 20 miles away. Towering above you to the west is the very imposing Dicks Peak and, to the southeast, Jacks Peak, both bearing patches of snow that will last throughout most of the year. The best viewpoint is actually just before the top of the pass on a flat rock to the south of the trail.

You've had your fun. Now 13.6 miles into your route, it is time for the long downhill to Dicks Lake. In the next 1.7 miles you drop about 900 feet via a number of switchbacks to a saddle above Dicks Lake. While the south-facing side of Dicks Pass is loaded with grasses and wildflowers growing in the volcanic soil and between the rocks, the north-facing side of fractured granite is dominated by thick stands of mountain hemlock with just a few grasses here and there. A north-facing slope near 9000′ elevation on the western side of the Sierra holds a tremendous amount of snow for much of the year. Thus the growing season is too short for

---

Sidetrip: Emerald Bay

A right turn at the junction east and above Dicks Lake will take you to Emerald Bay in 4.9 miles via the Bay View trail. Straight ahead, northwest, is a rock knob. With a quick scramble, you will discover tremendous views here. Fontanillis Lake and Dicks Peak can be seen respectively to the west and south.

---

most trees except the hardy hemlock. In addition, the hemlock is so prolific that it shades out the competition. At the saddle east of and above Dicks Lake you meet a junction.

A left at the saddle continues your TRT/PCT journey. After a 0.2-mile descent southeast, you reach a short spur trail south to Dicks Lake, a large lake with plenty of space along its shore to roam or camp. Tucked away on the shady north side of Dicks Peak, this lake may still be frozen over in July after a big winter. At about 15.5 miles from your trailhead, with about 17 easier miles to go, this locale may be a good one to spend the night. From the spur trail, your trail veers northwest and continues another 0.3 mile to Fontanillis Lake, one of my favorites. Exposed granite and a few scattered hardy trees surround Fontanillis Lake. The trail approaches the granite-lined lakeshore in about 0.3 mile, but takes another 0.3 mile to reach its shore. You hike in and out of numerous little bays, all with glorious views of Dicks Peak hulking above. Many great lunch and swimming spots are found along the way (perhaps a bit cold for a swim, but how

Sidetrip: Upper Velma Lake

For another interesting sidetrip, follow the creek you crossed as it falls down a steep granite slab almost 0.5 mile to Upper Velma Lake. The granite slab is steep enough that the water, which is usually quite shallow, cascades down the slope, but it is not too steep to prevent you from walking right next to the water. A trail runs from Upper Velma Lake to Middle Velma Lake, where you can rejoin the Tahoe Rim Trail, or head out to Emerald Bay.

about a quick jump in?). At the end of the lake, at 0.3 mile farther down, the trail crosses its outlet

Dicks Lake, Fontanillis (left background), and Middle Velma Lake (right background), from Dicks Pass.

creek (another tough early season crossing) and descends toward Middle Velma Lake.

After crossing Fontanillis Lake's outlet creek, you begin a descent through a deep forest of mostly red firs. In 0.8 mile of walking, and about 400 feet of descent, you reach a junction where the TRT heads left (west). A right turn would lead you out to Emerald Bay, about 5 miles away. On the TRT in a short distance you see Middle Velma Lake, a large lake with many islands that makes for a great camping or swimming spot, although like much of Desolation Wilderness, it can be quite popular in the summer. If you are continuing north, be aware that the next lake, Richardson Lake, is smaller and marshier. Its accessibility by 4-wheel drive vehicles makes it less attractive to those backpackers hoping to enjoy a motor-free experience.

Once you have relaxed or camped at Middle Velma Lake, 17.5 miles from the Echo Lakes trail-

185

head, you continue your journey north along the TRT/PCT. This second half of the hike from the Velma Lakes to Barker Pass is dramatically different than the first half that began at Echo Lake. While the first half goes through the heart of Desolation Wilderness, with more rocks than trees and beautiful rock-lined lakes (and lots of people), you are now embarking on a 15-mile journey through forest with only one lake (and fewer people). Before you leave Middle Velma Lake, be sure to filter water: the next reliable source is Richardson Lake 8.3 miles north.

Shortly after you leave Middle Velma Lake, you meet a junction, 0.3 mile past the previous one. Here a trail heads west down to Camper Flat and provides access to a whole host of Desolation Wilderness lakes and the Rubicon River. From this

---

Sidetrip: Meeks Bay

At this point, the Tahoe-Yosemite Trail parts company with the PCT/TRT. The Phipps Pass Trail would lead you about 12 miles to Meeks Bay (and the terminus of the TYT). Along the way, you pass Phipps Peak (9234′) and Rubicon, Stony Ridge, Shadow, Crag and Genevieve lakes. If you have been hiking all the way from Yosemite you are almost home. A wonderful point-to-point hike starts at Emerald Bay and ends at Meeks Bay via the Velma Lakes and Phipps Pass. This 18-mile route takes you by a string of lakes and exceptional viewpoints.

---

intersection the TRT/PCT/TYT turns north and in 0.3 mile crosses boggy lands bordering Middle Velma Lake's outlet creek. It then goes 0.9 mile gently uphill to a junction with the Phipps Pass Trail, which turns off to the right.

The TRT/PCT continues for the next 4.4 miles after the junction with the Phipps Pass Trail to a junction with a faint trail, which heads over to

Lake Genevieve. (This little-used trail is overgrown in many spots and is not recommended.) There are two important features along this 4.4-mile stretch. The first is seasonal Phipps Creek, reached after a 1.5-mile, mostly gentle descent. You could camp near it. The second is after a 2-mile, erratic ascent to a high point with a short spur trail west, from which you can survey the Rubicon River lands. Past this you descend 0.9 mile to the next trail junction. You pass several small meadows blooming with asters, Queen Anne's lace, groundsel, corn lilies and elephant heads. Thru-hikers are the primary users of this lightly used section of trail. If you meet someone who is hiking all the way from Mexico to Canada, be sure to take advantage of the opportunity and talk to them about their experiences. They have already walked over 1,100 miles and surely have some fascinating stories to tell. One thing is certain, if they have made it this far, they are persistent.

Beyond the junction with the trail to Lake Genevieve, the combined PCT/TRT begins by going downhill. You can enjoy the views of Mt. Tallac and Dicks Peak in the distance to the south. As the trail moves into a more densely forested area, you will be leaving Desolation Wilderness at its north boundary, about 1.5 miles past the junction. Then 0.75 mile north of the wilderness, traversing along the base of Lost Corner Mountain, you reach a minor saddle. Next, you head 0.7 mile down to the northwest corner of tree-lined Richardson Lake. This pleasant little lake has several nice campsites set among the trees, but look out for mosquitoes in the spring. Richardson Lake, about 6.7 miles from the Barker Pass trailhead, is accessible via a 4-wheel drive dirt road so be prepared for outdoor recreational vehicles, the main users of the north-shore campsites.

From Richardson Lake, the trail heads north, first descending the lower east slopes of Sourdough Hill, then proceeding west above Miller Meadows, beyond which it crosses two dirt roads. Just past the first road (about 2 miles from Richardson Lake) you cross Miller Creek, a good source of water and a potentially difficult creek to cross in the spring. The second road crossing, about 200 yards farther, is the very popular McKinney Rubicon OHV Trail, which heads east down to the McKinney Estates subdivision on the west shore of Lake Tahoe, or west on a famously difficult stretch of 4-wheel terrain to the Rubicon River.

Onward, your journey is pleasant as you pass through thick fir forest and occasional small meadows opulent with wildflowers. The gently rolling terrain heads northwest 1.5 miles to Bear Lake's outlet creek, then 0.4 farther up to the Bear Lake Road.

You cross the road and stay just above it for 0.4 mile, but just after both roads turn north, you can drop to the adjacent road and follow it about 200 yards to Barker Creek, with abundant space frequented by OHV campers. You now have a 2-mile long, 420-foot ascent to Forest Route 3. On it, you will pass several small streams that often supply water and promote wildflowers until the late summer. You slowly climb through Barker Meadows and eventually to Barker Pass. The trail ends on a major dirt road, Forest Route 3, which provides access through Blackwood Canyon to Lake Tahoe. The PCT/TRT from Barker Pass to Tahoe City begins across the road and slightly to the west.

Barker Pass to Tahoe City

(16.7 miles)

Difficulty—This moderate to strenuous section has several good-sized climbs, but more of the trail runs downhill than uphill. The starting elevation is 7650′ and it ends near the Truckee River at about 6300′. If you are starting from the Tahoe City end it is more strenuous.

Best Seasons—This section can usually be hiked from late-July to mid-October (or until the first major snow). Most of the first 7 miles of this trail section are at high elevations which receive a lot of snow. Much of the trail faces north or east—a combination which leads to a late snow melt.

Highlights—There are beautiful ridgeline views of Lake Tahoe, Granite Chief Wilderness, both Blackwood and Ward canyons, and lush areas loaded with wildflowers in both canyons. Twin Peaks (8878′), a Sierra crest landmark, is accessible from the trail. In addition, there are numerous little stream crossings and several good camping spots. A lovely little waterfall cascades near one part of the trail in upper Ward Canyon. There is a very pretty series of meadows known as Page Meadows, although on some maps it is listed as "Paige." A dense forest area with huge pines and firs grows in the Ward Creek watershed. Wildlife is abundant and includes bear, coyote, raccoon, blue grouse, and perhaps goshawk and spotted owls. Hopefully you will be lucky enough to spot them. Between Barker Pass and Twin Peaks this lakeless stretch tends to get less use than the trails in the Desolation Wilderness area which has mountain lakes.

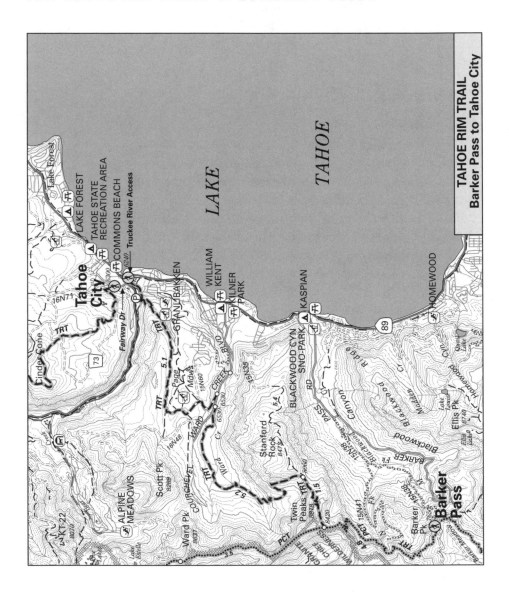

However, in the Page Meadows vicinity, bikers, hikers and joggers abound. At the end of your trip you may find the Truckee River is a perfect place to swim or to complete your day with a rafting trip down the Truckee.

Heads Up!—In the fall, as streams dry up, the water supply can be limited. You reach the North Fork of Blackwood Creek, about 2.5 miles north of Barker Pass at the bottom of a meadow. In the next mile, you may find one or more springs before late summer. However, the most dependable water source is Ward Creek, about 8.5 miles north of Barker Pass. You parallel the creek, sometimes at a distance, for over 3 miles, and by the time you're starting north from the canyon's main road you have only 5 miles to the Tahoe City trailhead.

The only places to swim are the Truckee River at your destination, and at adjacent Lake Tahoe. The Commons public beach is about 0.25 mile east of the Tahoe Rim Trail on Highway 28 in the center of Tahoe City. There are lots of junctions and turnoffs on this section of trail and the Forest Service has been closing and rebuilding roads and trails in this area, so follow the TRT trail markers and pay attention to where you are going.

Tips for Mountain Bikers—The first five miles of the TRT overlap with the PCT. As you know by now, bikes are not allowed on the PCT. From Twin Peaks to Tahoe City, bikes are allowed: Start at "64 Acres" in Tahoe City (also known as the Truckee River Access Parking Lot) and follow the TRT along the Truckee River, then head uphill rather steeply. In some places there are lots of loose rocks. After 1.7 miles, you reach the east edge of the Page Meadows area and a whole network of great biking trails. The TRT turns right at the first major junction (to the left, a trail crosses a small meadow and heads uphill into the trees), and provides a great gentle

191

uphill ride through the forest above the perimeter of the meadows. In another 1.3 miles, you reach another junction where you have two riding options:

Alternative Routes—Turn left and follow the TRT as it skirts the edge of a meadow and crosses another one. The section of trail is built-up six inches above the meadow to protect the fragile ecosystem. After passing Page Meadows, the trail heads into the woods. At first the TRT follows a moderate downhill course, then descends more steeply on an old dirt road to Ward Creek Road, a major paved thoroughfare. Turn right on Ward Creek Road, and go uphill 0.2 mile to where you will reconnect with the TRT on your left.

The alternative route to Ward Creek Boulevard and the TRT is to continue ahead for about 1 mile to the next major junction. Turn left and enjoy a fun downhill to Chamonix Road, a paved street in the Alpine Peaks subdivision. Take Chamonix downhill to Courchevel, turn left, and head downhill. In a little more than 1 mile, you will see the Tahoe Rim Trail on your right. (Along the way the road name changes from Courchevel to Ward Creek Boulevard.) From Ward Creek Blvd., the TRT follows an old dirt road for about two miles to a washed-out bridge. After the bridge, the trail starts uphill in earnest through a beautiful area of small meadows where aspens are interspersed with forests of tall old-growth trees. As the trail gets steeper, most bikers will walk their bikes or stop and turn around. Eventually, about 5.2 miles beyond Ward Creek Boulevard you reach a saddle between Twin Peaks on your right and Stanford Rock on the left. The trail to the right leads steeply uphill to Twin Peaks where bikes are not allowed. The trail to the left leads uphill to a great lookout point, and then a 4-mile, fun downhill on a dirt road to Ward Creek

Boulevard. Just before reaching the road, you cross Ward Creek in an area that can be deep and difficult to ford until late summer. The 4-mile section between Stanford Rock and Ward Creek is also a challenging but beautiful uphill ride. The start is about 0.5 mile east of the TRT on Ward Creek Road. You will see a gated trail leading off from the road next to a large open flat area on the south side of the highway. Immediately after passing the gate you will need to cross Ward Creek. The climb varies between moderately steep to very steep, and provides tremendous views of the lake and Blackwood Canyon. Eventually you reach the Stanford Rock viewpoint and a spectacular view of Ward Canyon, Twin Peaks and the Sierra crest. After enjoying the view, turn left and follow the trail downhill to a junction with the Tahoe Rim Trail. Or, you can turn around and ride back the way you came. If you choose to ride from here on the TRT, be prepared for a challenging and steep ride on loose soil, with several technical rocky sections.

Getting There, Barker Pass to Tahoe City—Take Highway 89 (West Lake Blvd.) about 4.25 miles south of Tahoe City and turn right onto the Blackwood Canyon Road, starting opposite Kaspian Beach. Drive 7 miles to the crest above Blackwood Canyon to where the paved road turns to dirt, then another 0.2 mile to the Pacific Crest Trail trailhead parking lot on your right; it is a dirt lot.

Getting There, Tahoe City to Barker Pass—From the intersection of Highway 89 and Highway 28 at the stoplight in Tahoe City, head south on Highway 89 0.25 mile to the Truckee River Access Parking Area (64 Acres). Park in the lot. The trail starts along the south side of the Truckee River. As you follow the Truckee River west and downstream the trail begins as a bike trail. Continue to follow the river downstream as the bike trail leads into a

193

Volcanic formation north of Barker Pass.

paved road that then becomes a dirt road. Walk on the dirt road for 0.3 mile and meet a gate right next to the Truckee River. Go around the gate and across a south-climbing gravel road to the start of the Tahoe Rim Trail.

Trail Description

At Barker Pass (7650') the trail begins by traversing west around the south side of Barker Peak (8166'), where you get excellent views of Desolation Wilderness to the south. In 0.9 mile your moderately steep walk through a field of mule ears reaches the Sierra crest, where you will have views east down the expanse of Blackwood Canyon to Lake Tahoe. Beyond the crest, your route continues with a gentle ascent northeast across the canyon's upper slopes. In 0.25 mile you pass a beautiful stream bordered with aster, delphinium, tiger lily, columbine, paintbrush, and other wildflowers.

After a pleasant walk gently up through mostly open volcanic terrain that is interrupted by a red fir forest, you cross a steep face to the base of two lofty volcanic plugs, about 0.5 mile past the stream. From here you have wide open views of Lake Tahoe and Blackwood Canyon to the east. From these lofty twin rock formations, the trail descends into a large bowl lush with wildflowers and greenery late into the summer. Mountain hemlock is now the dominant tree. These fascinating trees are laden with cones on their thick green foliage. The hemlock can be most easily identified by the drooping top of the tree, which gives it a fairy-tale appearance.

As you descend farther into this lovely bowl, you pass several areas graced by Sierra wildflowers including explorer's gentian, which blooms into the fall. At the bottom of the bowl, about 2.5 miles from the trailhead, is a great camping spot. It has a running stream (North Fork of Blackwood Creek), a nice flat place to rest your head, and views of Lake Tahoe and Blackwood Canyon. Just beyond this camping spot, the trail rounds a corner and continues to descend past several spring-fed creeks. After about a 1-mile traverse from the camping spot, your trail starts a series of long switchbacks almost to the crest of the ridge. The climb begins in a dark viewless forest of large red fir trees. As you climb, you will see Ellis Peak to the southeast, Desolation Wilderness to the south, and almost all of Blackwood Canyon to the east. Just below the top of the crest, you round the ridge to find new views of the south side of Twin Peaks (8878'). Then you pass the Granite Chief Wilderness sign and quickly reach the Sierra crest, where there are views in all directions. To your north and west, you can see the full expanse of Granite Chief Wilderness, to the northeast, you see nearby Twin Peaks, to the east Lake Tahoe, and to the south Desolation Wilderness lies in the distance. In the foreground you can

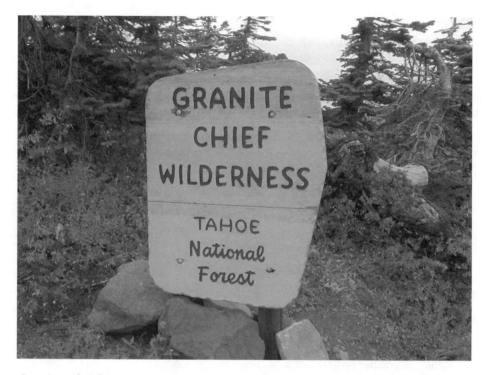

Granite Chief Wilderness boundary near Twin Peaks.

review the knife-edge ridge whose backside you just climbed.

Just 0.25 mile beyond this exposed viewpoint you meet a junction, at 4.8 miles from Barker Pass. This is where the Tahoe Rim Trail and Pacific Crest Trail part ways after running together for a total of about 50 miles. Straight ahead are the PCT and Canada. A right turn takes you along the southern slope of Twin Peaks on the Tahoe Rim Trail. Those of you without the time or inclination to hike to Canada, should turn right. In 0.5 mile you meet a spur trail to the top of the eastern Twin Peak. (For those hiking south, this is about 6.2 miles from the Ward Canyon trailhead.) If you are going to take this trail, be forewarned that it can be a bit treacherous, but the views are spectacular. A safer route is to head directly up to the saddle separating the two summits. From the summit trail junction, continue descending along a ridgeline on the TRT for 1 mile through a mixed forest of red fir, hemlock, and western white pine to a saddle. Along the route you will find scenic views of Squaw Valley and Alpine Meadows to the north. At the saddle you meet another junction. The Tahoe Rim Trail turns left, while the trail straight ahead would take you to Stanford Rock, as described in the mountain biking section.

You are now heading north down a rather steep hill through a deep forest of fir and hemlock trees into Ward Canyon. This portion of the trail is bone-jarringly steep with loose dark soil, but the views are glorious, especially of Twin Peaks to your left. After about 1.1 miles of downhill, you encounter a large meadow at the base of Twin Peaks. This beautiful meadow surrounded with imposing peaks high above is a splendid resting spot. Next, the descent is less steep and takes you into a more thinly forested section. You pass another meadow and then see a waterfall just off the trail on your left. This unnamed waterfall is called McCloud Falls by some locals.

You will switchback down toward Ward Creek for 0.9 mile, and then pass several lush meadows that are surrounded by aspen trees, as well as large red firs and Jeffrey pines. You traverse above the creek to its crossing. Ward Creek can be wet and deep in the early summer and you may need to look around and find the best method. Once you cross the creek, your trail climbs briefly upstream and then turns right along a former road, which first traverses over 0.5 mile, and then heads gently downhill. You pass a washed-out bridge across a tributary of Ward Creek and the trail joins an old dirt road. You can camp just past the bridge site, to the north of the road, in an opening in the trees. Used as a Forest Service camp when they were building the Tahoe Rim Trail between here and

197

Pacific Crest from below Twin Peaks.

Twin Peaks, you can usually find water in the creek, or in a spring on the northeast edge of the camp.

The TRT, which is now an old dirt road arching eastward, heads gently downslope for 1.75 miles through meadows and forest to a trailhead on Ward Creek Boulevard, a paved road leading up to Alpine Peaks, a development on the "backside" (south) of Alpine Meadows Ski Area. Along this stretch of trail there are several nice views, including one of Grouse Rock, which you can see from a particularly pretty meadow that borders Ward Creek on your right. (Grouse Rock is the large volcanic rock on the ridgeline to the west between Twin Peaks and Ward Peak that sits right above the Pacific Crest Trail. It is a popular destination with backcountry skiers.) Your trail, blocked at the trailhead by a gate, was once used regularly as an off-highway vehicle route. In the great New Year floods of 1997, the road was washed-out in several locations. Where it was once smooth dirt, the trail in many locations became a jumble of rocks where the soil washed away.

At Ward Creek Boulevard you see a Tahoe Rim Trail kiosk. Turn right (east) and walk 0.2 mile to the northwest-climbing road on the left. You now have 5 miles to go to the Tahoe City trailhead. Take this gated dirt road, as it climbs steeply away from Ward Creek Boulevard, through a thick forest of white fir and Jeffrey pine. Near the top of the hill, Ward Canyon, Ward Peak and the Sherwood Chairlift at Alpine Meadows Ski Area can be viewed through an opening in the trees. After a steep 0.6 mile, the trail levels at a junction with another dirt road. A right turn here would take you to eastern Page Meadows and the Talmont Estates development in about 1 mile. The TRT angles left and winds up through a young forest for 0.4 mile to the road's end, where posts were installed to block vehicles. Here a lateral trail heads left to the lowest of the Page Meadows and provides access to the Alpine Peaks neighborhood about 0.25 mile away.

Sidetrip: Oven

Just off this lateral trail is an oven built by Basque sheepherders. Built in the 1950s, the oven provides evidence of a unique lifestyle once present in Page Meadows. Sit next to the oven and imagine sheepherders enjoying fresh baked bread while watching sheep graze in the meadow under the beautiful aspen trees.

You are now in the Page Meadows area, a series of five interconnected meadows that serve as a popular retreat for hiking, mountain biking and cross-country skiing. The meadows provide an easily accessible outdoor haven for many residents

Twin Peaks from Ward Canyon.

who live in developments close by. They are especially popular as a place to go cross-country skiing on full moon nights.

From the lateral trail west the TRT goes straight ahead through the road gate and follows the meadow area on your left for a short distance before entering a large meadow. The trail is built up six inches above the meadow to prevent damage to this fragile ecosystem. About a third of the way across this beautiful meadow, you meet a trail starting east. This provides access to three other large meadows, as well as a route to Tahoe City. The TRT continues straight. At the end of the meadow, turn around to enjoy a tree-framed view of Twin Peaks. Your trail now heads north out of the meadow, into a grove of aspens before entering a forest of fir trees. About 0.2 mile from the meadow you meet another junction.

Sidetrip: Alpine Meadows

At the junction just mentioned, a spur trail leads left (west). In about 2 miles you would reach the Alpine Meadows residential area. In addition, spurs from this trail lead to the top of Scott Peak, the Alpine Meadows Ski Area, or Tahoe City via the bike trail along the Truckee River. These trails are challenging mountain biking routes or pleasant hikes through the forest.

The TRT turns right (east), however, and parallels the mostly unseen meadows on your right. The next 1.3 miles are primarily downhill, with several short uphills. This is a very popular mountain biking section for good reason. It rolls along with lots of fun little twists and turns on a fairly smooth surface. The trail levels near the edge of a small meadow and you meet another junction.

Sidetrip: Rawhide Drive

The right turn leads across a snippet of meadow and then after a short uphill, it runs into a major trail. Turn left and in 1.5 downhill miles, you reach Rawhide Drive, close to Tahoe City. If you want to head toward Tahoe City at this point, follow Rawhide north to Granlibakken Road, turn right here and follow Granlibakken Road to West Lake Boulevard, also known as Highway 89. Turn left on the bike trail and in 0.5 mile you will be in Tahoe City. A right-hand turn on this trail junction will take you to the biggest meadow in the Page Meadows area in 0.5 mile.

The TRT turns left (east) and begins a 0.6-mile steep descent down a narrow canyon, with rocky and challenging (for bikes) terrain, to a junction. The Tahoe Rim Trail veers left. If you are on your bike and would like to avoid this difficult section, refer to the sidetrip above for an easier route to Tahoe City. From the TRT marker you travel almost

1 mile, generally downhill, winding through the shade of the fir trees until you arrive at a trail junction on the Truckee River. Turn right and follow the trail 0.1 mile east to a gravel road where the trail tread ends.You now walk across the road and past a gate. Stop here to swim in the Truckee River or to watch summer rafters. Your trail is now a dirt road heading along the river upstream 0.3 mile to a paved road. The National Forest 64 Acres (Truckee River Access) parking lot is straight ahead.

From the parking lot, a 0.3-mile walk along bike paths and roads reaches the beginning of the next section of the Tahoe Rim Trail, from Tahoe City to Brockway Summit. Follow the bike trail to the pedestrian bridge across the Truckee River to Highway 89. Turn right, and follow the bike trail 50 yards to its end. Cross Highway 89 to Fairway Drive, which is directly across the highway. Go 0.2 mile up Fairway Drive to the Fairway Community Center parking lot on your right. The Tahoe Rim Trail continues across the street.

CHAPTER SEVEN

Other Tahoe Area Attractions

Once you have exhausted all of the recreation possibilities on the Tahoe Rim Trail, you may want to check out some other Tahoe area trails. Brief summaries of a few of my favorites are presented below. To obtain more information on the hikes and rides, take a look at some of the books listed in "Recommended Reading." Jeffrey Schaffer's *The Tahoe Sierra*, also published by Wilderness Press, includes information on all of the hikes listed.

Hiking

Emerald Bay

Difficulty—Easy. Depending on where you go, it is anywhere from 2 to 9 miles.

Map—Tahoe Rim Trail Map 2, Section 7.

Best Seasons—Do this hike in early spring, or later in the fall. After a mild winter, you can hike it from April through December.

Highlights—Emerald Bay provides many great hiking opportunities. On the edge of a beautiful sandy beach at the western edge of the bay is the Vikingsholm Castle with its granite touches, carved wood spikes and gargoyles, roof covered with wild-flowers, and its gorgeous stained-glass windows. The castle was constructed in 1928-1929 by Mrs. Lora Knight, after she had purchased 239 acres at the end of Emerald Bay for $250,000. Trails lead from the Vikingsholm to a beautiful waterfall, and along both sides of Emerald Bay.

Heads Up!—During the summer, these trails (especially the 1-mile portion from the parking lot to the Vikingsholm) can be very busy! The best time to go is on a weekday in early spring or late fall, when you are more likely to have the place to yourself.

Getting There—From Tahoe City, drive 17 miles south on Highway 89 to the Vikingsholm parking lot located on the south side of the road (10 miles north of the intersection of Highway 50 and Highway 89 in South Lake Tahoe). During the summer, this lot can be full early in the day. An alternative parking area is located one-quarter mile farther south on Highway 89 at the Eagle Falls Trailhead. There is a fee to use this lot.

Brief Trail Description—The trail from the parking lot to the Vikingsholm is a gentle descent for a mile. Two trails lead out from the Vikingsholm. The first takes you 1.5 miles along the north side of Emerald Bay, in and out of sandy inlets, past the Emerald Bay Boat Campground, to Emerald Point. This south-facing section of trail is the first area to emerge from the winter snows. From Emerald Point, the trail continues across a small peninsula and heads north for 3 miles along the lakeshore to Bliss State Park (along the way keep your eyes open for ospreys and eagles).

A second trail leaves the Vikingsholm, and heads southwest a short distance to a junction at a bridge across Eagle Creek. A right turn will lead you up to Eagle Falls in a third of a mile. The falls are quite dramatic when filled with springtime runoff. If you make a left turn, you will cross Eagle Creek and travel past the Emerald Bay landslide of 1955, then along the southern side of the bay to Emerald Bay Campground, 1.5 miles from the Vikingsholm.

Loch Leven Lakes

Difficulty—It is a moderately difficult, but well-graded climb to the first of the three Loch Leven Lakes. The journey between the lakes is an easy ascent. If you visit all the lakes and return, it is a total distance of a little less than 8 miles.

Best Seasons—Late-June to late-October. The trail is at a relatively low elevation (5880'), but faces north in an area that receives much snow.

Highlights—This hike is 30 miles closer to the Bay Area and Sacramento than most other Sierra hikes. It is also easily accessible via Interstate 80. In just a few miles you can reach three wonderful lakes lying on granite benches. The two farthest lakes provide good camping opportunities and excellent swimming in relatively warm water. These lakes make especially attractive locations for family camping trips, since they are great to explore and easy enough to get to for many families.

Heads Up!—The easy accessibility of this trail make Loch Leven Lakes busy places throughout the summer. You will almost certainly not have the lakes to yourself.

Getting There—Take Interstate 80 to the Big Bend Exit, which is 1.5 miles east of Cisco Grove, and 6 miles west of Soda Springs. Drive about 1 mile south on Hampshire Rocks Road (Old Highway 40), past the Rainbow Lodge, and park on the right at the trailhead parking lot. It has a pit toilet and parking space for about ten vehicles.

205

Brief Trail Description—The trail is a pleasant woodsy walk up past several streams bordered by wildflowers, before it crosses a railroad track. At that point, it begins a moderate, well-graded climb through a thick forest of firs and pines. In just under 3 miles from the trailhead, you reach Upper Loch Leven Lake, followed in 0.3 mile by Middle Loch Leven Lake, and then at 3.9 miles from the trailhead, my favorite of the three, High Loch Leven Lake.

Winnemucca Lake/Round Top Lake

Difficulty—Easy to moderately difficult. This is a fairly short hike, only 2.5 miles to Winnemucca Lake and 3.4 miles to Round Top Lake, with a round-trip distance of 6.8 miles. The high elevation of this trail may make it moderately difficult for those not accustomed to high altitudes. The trail starts at 8590' with Round Top Lake sitting at 9350' elevation. A faint trail also leads from Round Top Lake up a very steep mile to the top of Round Top (10,381'). If you add Round Top to your itinerary, this hike is strenuous.

Best Seasons—Late-July through October. This hike is in a high elevation area that receives a tremendous amount of snow that can last till mid-summer.

Highlights—If you are looking for relatively easy access to some tremendous high mountain scenery, this is a great choice. An incredible variety of wildflowers can be viewed between Carson Pass and Winnemucca Lake from late July through August. The prolific flower display may include lupine, elephant head, gentian, delphinium, monkeyflower, tiger lily, columbine, rein orchid, and a full palate of different colored paintbrush. The area around Round Top lake and mountain has a rugged appeal, and is a popular destination for summertime skiers and snowboarders, trying to find that last patch of snow. This hike is a good choice for those in the South Lake Tahoe area, only about 25 miles away.

Heads Up!—Permits are required to camp in the Mokelumne Wilderness Area, where much of this hike takes place. During the summer, permits can be obtained at the trailhead at Carson Pass. During the rest of the year, you need to contact the Amador Ranger District in Jackson, California at (209) 295-4251. Given the short distance to the lakes, and the fragility of this high-altitude location, it is best to dayhike this trail.

Getting There—The trail starts from Carson Pass near Kirkwood Ski Area south of Lake Tahoe. From Meyers, take Highway 89 south about 11 miles to the intersection of Highway 88 and 89 (Picketts Junction). Be sure to come to a complete stop at this remote intersection as the California Highway Patrol watches it closely. Turn right on Highway 88 and go approximately 9 miles through Hope Valley and up to Carson Pass. A parking area is on your left just as the road reaches the summit. An information center is at the trailhead (summers only).

Brief Trail Description—From the Carson Pass parking lot, your route is a gentle-to-moderate ascent for 2.5 miles to Winnemucca Lake. You will pass incredible summertime wildflower displays in the open areas below Winnemucca Lake. A mile farther of moderate climbing brings you to Round Top Lake, which sits in a basin just below huge rocky crags and Round Top (10,381'). From here you can follow a faint very steep trail to the top of Round Top, where you will find 360-degree, awe-inspiring views. Your views to the north include Lake Tahoe, and a number of high peaks surrounding it,

207

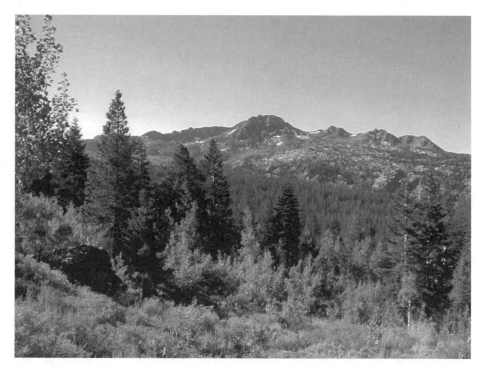

Round Top from Carson Pass.

including Freel Peak (10,881'), Mt. Tallac (9735'), Pyramid Peak (9983') and on a clear day, Mount Rose (10,776'), some 46 miles away. The last few hundred feet at the top of the mountain is steep, crumbly volcanic rock. I recommend stopping where the ridgetop trail meets the steep rock, for equally spectacular views without the added danger.

Crag Lake

Difficulty—Easy to moderately difficult.

Map—Tahoe Rim Trail Map 2, Section 7.

Best Seasons—Mid-June to mid-October. This trail provides late spring access to eastern Desolation Wilderness.

Highlights: Crag Lake is an especially magnificent spot with the high granite slab of Crag Peak looming over the lake. This hike is the easiest route into Desolation Wilderness from the Tahoe basin, and it usually is snow free a month earlier than Eagle Falls, Bay View, and Echo Lake, the other Tahoe area trailheads used to access Desolation Wilderness. Both lakes are great locations for swimming or camping.

Heads Up!—This trail is quite popular for both day-hiking and camping so parking can be limited in the summer. A permit is required to enter Desolation Wilderness. Day permits can be obtained at the trailhead, for backpacking permits contact the Forest Service office in South Lake Tahoe at (530) 573-2694.

Getting There—From Tahoe City, drive 10 miles south on Highway 89 to Meeks Bay (this is about 17 miles north of the intersection of Highway 50 and Highway 89 at the South Lake Tahoe "Y"). The trailhead is on the west side of Highway 89 at the bend in the road.

Brief Trail Description—This trail starts out as a level walk through widely scattered forest and a wildflower-dotted meadow, and then heads up into the trees following the path of Meeks Creek. In 4.6 miles you reach Genevieve Lake, and Crag Lake shortly thereafter. If you would like to hike farther, you can continue past Stony Ridge Lake and Rubicon Lake, before heading over Phipps Pass to the Tahoe Rim Trail and Middle Velma Lake. From Middle Velma Lake, Emerald Bay is just 5 miles away, making a spectacular 18 mile point-to-point hike.

Fontanillis/Velma Loop

Difficulty—Strenuous, 12-mile loop with 2000 feet of elevation gain.

Map—Tahoe Rim Trail Map 2, Section 7.

Best Seasons—Mid-July to early October

Highlights—Here is Desolation Wilderness in all its splendor, with spectacular views of granite peaks, mountain lakes and a variety of plantlife. Eagle, Granite, Fontanillis, and Dicks lakes, as well as all three Velma Lakes, are excellent for swimming or camping.

Heads Up!—These trails, especially on the first mile to Eagle Lake, can be crowded in the summer. Day use and backpacking permits are required. Day-use permits can be obtained at the trailhead. To get a backpacking permit contact the Forest Service office at (530) 573-2694.

Getting There—You can start from either of two trailheads, both are located at the western end of Emerald Bay on Highway 89. The Eagle Lake/Eagle Falls trailhead is about 200 yards south of the Vikingsholm parking lot, which is about 17 miles south of Tahoe City, and 10 miles north of South Lake Tahoe. There is a $3.00 fee for parking. The Bay View campground/trailhead is 1 mile south of the Eagle Falls trailhead on Highway 89, across from the vista parking area. Drive through the campground to its western edge where you will find trailhead parking.

Brief Trail Description—The Eagle Lake trail ascends about 1 mile to often crowded Eagle Lake. Then you stay left and climb steadily, and sometimes steeply, along the slope of south Maggies Peak to a junction 2.6 miles from the trailhead. If you are starting from the Bay View trailhead, you hike about 0.5 mile to a stunning view of Emerald Bay, and then another half mile to Granite Lake. Next is a steep set of switchbacks into the cleavage between Maggies Peaks (these breast-shaped mountains, also known as Round Buttons, were named after Maggie's breasts. Who was Maggie? Legend has it that she was a buxom barmaid at the Tahoe Tavern Resort in the late 1800s). Your Bay View trail reaches the saddle between the two peaks then descends to a junction, and a meeting with the Eagle Lake trail. From here, with both trails as one, you hike along rolling rocky terrain for a little less than a mile to a junction, where you take a left turn onto the trail leading to Dicks Lake. Now in the heart of the stark Desolation Wilderness, land of granite boulders, sandy soils and scattered trees, you go about 0.5 mile to a beautiful pond. This shallow body of water is a good swimming spot, and is especially pretty in the fall when the mountain heather which surrounds the lake turns bright red. Your journey ascends across a granite slab to a saddle and junction. A left turn climbs up to Dicks Pass, and a right turn takes you to Dicks and Fontanillis Lakes. You are now on the Tahoe Rim Trail/Pacific Crest Trail (For more detailed information on the next two miles of trail refer to the Tahoe Rim Trail description in Chapter 6). In 0.2 mile you meet another junction, with a left turn going to Dicks Lake in 100 yards, and a right turn heading to Fontanillis, your next destination. The trail follows along Fontanillis Lake and finally reaches its outlet creek.

The trail crosses the creek and heads downhill for about a mile along a ridge line to a junction. If you turn left, you will be heading to Middle Velma Lake on the Pacific Crest Trail/Tahoe Rim Trail. However, you should turn right, leave the TRT/PCT, and head uphill for a little over a mile back to the Dicks Lake junction, and then retrace your steps back to the Bay View/Eagle Falls trail junction. Hopefully, you left a car at both trailheads, which will enable you to hike a loop back to Emerald Bay via a different trail than where you began.

Donner to Squaw Valley

Difficulty—A strenuous hike of about 15 miles.

Best Seasons—Mid-July to mid-October. Patches of snow can last until August on the north-facing slope of Anderson Peak.

Highlights—This section of the Pacific Crest Trail provides miles of stunning 360-degree views from atop a windswept ridge. Ridgecrest views reach all the way from Mount Rose in the northeast, to Lake Tahoe, in the southeast, with the Granite Chief Wilderness to the south and west. You will see a wide variety of terrain and wildflower species, including large fields of mule ears. This well-constructed trail has firm-packed sandy soils good for fast-moving, long-distance hikers or runners. All will enjoy its high-altitude remoteness. When Desolation Wilderness is packed with people, you may only encounter a few people on this trail. The trail goes by Roller Pass, a portion of the original Emigrant Trail used by pioneers when they came to California.

Heads Up!—Very little water is available on the trail, and if hiking in late summer or fall, assume that there will be no water. Early in the summer, a northeast-facing 100-foot-long section of trail about 3 miles into the trail may be treacherous if it is still covered with snow. Most of the trail is treeless and exposed to the sun and wind; be sure to bring plenty of sunscreen and a windbreaker. Your trail intersects with a variety of use paths descending from Shirley Canyon in the last mile of your route. Take care to avoid getting lost.

Getting There—Take Interstate 80 to the Soda Springs exit and drive four miles east on Highway 40 to Donner Summit (Sugar Bowl Academy will be on your right). Take a right turn at the summit, just before the road starts to go downhill, and go 0.2 mile to the trailhead on your left. This point-to-point hike requires a shuttle: be sure to leave a vehicle in Squaw Valley.

Brief Trail Description—Climb south on the Pacific Crest Trail, where in 1 mile you reach a junction with the Mt. Judah Loop trail. This alternate route heads up to Mt. Judah, which has excellent views, and then circles back and meets the PCT, adding 0.4 miles to your hike's length. About 2 miles into the hike you reach a saddle, Roller Pass. Just off the trail to the southeast, the Donner Party of 1846 winched their wagons up the steep slope below. Another 0.3 mile of gentle climbing brings you to another saddle below Mt. Lincoln. From here, the trail traverses across a steep slope, and then follows the ridgecrest with views in all directions for several miles to Anderson Peak. Your trail circles Anderson Peak, than climbs another ridge for a 1-mile journey to Tinker Knob, where a short use trail takes you to its summit.

At 8 miles into your hike, the trail now descends from Tinker Knob into a deep wide bowl (North Fork of American River Canyon) with wildflowers and sparse tree cover. You cross this bowl and then begin a steady climb, and at 4 miles from Tinker Knob, you reach a junction. Head east (left) on a steady downhill for 3 miles into Squaw Valley, where you will end the trail next to the Squaw Valley Fire Station.

Aloha Lake Loop via Tamarack Trail

Difficulty—This 12-mile loop is strenuous overall. The first 2.5 miles are very strenuous.

Map—Tahoe Rim Trail Map 1, Section 7.

Best Seasons—Mid-July through Mid-October.

Highlights—This is a classic hike into the heart of Desolation Wilderness with views of over a dozen lakes, numerous high granite and volcanic peaks, and a tremendous variety of mountain terrain.

Heads Up!—The first few miles up a canyon to a saddle are very steep, with almost 2000 feet of elevation gain. While not mountain climbing, it is certainly one of the steepest sections of trail I have ever hiked. It is especially difficult if you are carrying a heavy backpack. In the early summer this steep section can be icy and will require extra caution.

Getting There—Go about 0.5 mile west of Camp Richardson on Highway 89 and turn south on Fallen Leaf Lake Road (this is about 3 miles northwest of the intersection of Highway 50 and 89 in South Lake Tahoe). Follow this road 5.3 miles along the edge of Fallen Leaf Lake to the Glen Alpine Trailhead. The first 4.5 miles of the route are one and one-half lanes wide, and the last 0.8 miles is only one lane wide. From the Glen Alpine parking area, walk on Fallen Leaf Lake Road back towards the lake about 0.25 mile to the Tamarack trail on the right-hand (south) side.

Brief Trail Description—Hike 2.5 steep miles to a level junction with the Triangle Lake trail. These first few miles are extremely beautiful. You will hike through lush, almost jungle-like stream crossings with tiger lilies and columbines, and then climb through open areas of granite boulders from which you can enjoy great views. From the Triangle Lake junction go straight and climb more gently now to an open, almost treeless, viewpoint that faces Echo Lakes and Ralston Peak. Then, proceed downhill to a junction where the Tahoe Rim Trail/Pacific Crest Trail climbs up from Echo Lakes. Turn right on the PCT/TRT and follow the signs to Lake Aloha. For a more detailed description of the next 6 miles of trail along the Tahoe Rim Trail, refer to Section 7.

When you reach Lake Aloha, turn right, and head north along Aloha's eastern shore to a junction at its northern edge, where you turn right. In the next two miles you descend past two beautiful lakes, Heather and Susie. From Susie Lake you hike about 0.5 mile to a junction where you turn right. Now leaving the PCT/TRT you hike 0.5 mile to another junction, turn right, and follow it 3.3 miles, mostly downhill, to the Glen Alpine Trailhead where your car is parked.

Mountain Biking

Page Meadows/Ward Canyon

Difficulty—This area has a whole system of interconnected trails, which vary from easy to strenuous.

Map—Tahoe Rim Trail Map, Section 8.

Best Seasons—Late-June through late-October. Do not ride through the meadows when they are wet.

Highlights—These trails have it all: rolling forested terrain, lush green meadows in the summer, and glorious yellow and red leaves in the fall. It is a fun, smooth single-track trail with good climbs and thrilling descents. The variety of trails encourages you to visit again and again.

Heads Up!—The meadow areas are fragile when wet and should be avoided. Sometimes the elaborate trail network can be confusing. You may end up coming out somewhere different than you think, but that's part of the fun.

Getting There—Five different locations can be used to access this great network of dirt roads and single-track trails.

1) **Granlibakken Road:** Go 0.5 mile south of Tahoe City on Highway 89, turn right on Granlibakken Road, then left on Rawhide which you take to its end. The trail starts behind a gate.

2) **End of Silvertip in Talmont Estates:** Take Highway 89 two miles south of Tahoe City and turn right on Pine Street. Then turn right on Tahoe Park Heights, right on Big Pine, and left on Silvertip, which you follow to its end.

3) **Ward Canyon Boulevard:** Go south from Tahoe City about 2.5 miles on Highway 89. Turn right on Pineland Drive. At the end of the straightaway, veer left and follow the "Ward Canyon" sign. Go about 1 mile and take the dirt road on your right side that you will see continuing on past a gate.

4) **Chamonix:** Follow the directions to #3 above, and go an additional mile on Ward Canyon Boulevard, which becomes Courchevel. Turn right on Chamonix and go to the end of the road where a trail heads west.

5) **Snowcrest Road, Alpine Meadows:** Take Highway 89 3.5 miles north from Tahoe City to Alpine Meadows Road, where you turn left. Go about 1 mile and turn left on Snowcrest. Follow this road to a gated dirt road on your left.

Brief Trail Description—With so many different entrances and a complicated network of trails, exact directions are not offered here. A number of looping trails exist that go around Page Meadows, up to the top of Scott Peak at Alpine Meadows, or into the Tahoe City/Rawhide Area. One loop starts at Rawhide, goes over to Snowcrest and then back along the bike trail between Alpine Meadows and Tahoe City. Another trail starts at Chamonix and goes around the meadows, then loops back to the same starting point, or down to the Ward Canyon Boulevard. Explore the area and see where you end up.

Tahoe Cross Country Ski Area/ Burton Creek State Park

Difficulty—Moderate. A variety of trails and loops provide opportunities for all riders from beginners to expert.

Map—Tahoe Rim Trail Map, Section 1.

Best Seasons—Late-June through November, or up to the first major snow. After mild winters with less than average snow, it is possible to access this area by late May.

Highlights—A gently rolling open forest makes for great riding on smooth trails. You will find beautiful meadows and several excellent lakeviews at the top of the climbs.

Heads Up!—It's easy to get lost in the confusing trail pattern here. This is a busy area so watch out for hikers, dogs, children, horses and bears.

Getting There—From Tahoe City, take Highway 28 about 2.5 miles northeast to Fabian Way and turn left. Turn right on Village and proceed to the top of the hill, where Village veers right. Quickly turn left on Country Club Drive, and left again into the Tahoe Cross Country ski area parking lot.

Brief Trail Description—From the Nordic center, go up the dirt road heading west. This area has dozens of miles of trails that go to Tahoe City, Truckee, Northstar, or Brockway Summit. Mt. Watson is located at about 8 miles of steady climbing from the Nordic center where you'll have great lakeviews. Most trails are easy to moderate and very fun to ride. The opportunities for different rides are almost endless. For a detailed description of the Tahoe Rim Trail portion of this trail system, refer to the trail description for Section 1.

Flume Trail/Tahoe Rim Trail loop

Difficulty—Strenuous. 23 mile round-trip with a lot of climbing. The Flume Trail portion, which is 4.5 miles long, is on the edge of a cliff and may give the agrophobically challenged the "weebee jeebees."

Map—Tahoe Rim Trail Map, Section 3.

Best Seasons—Mid-June through October.

Highlights—This is one of the most spectacular mountain biking routes in the United States. The views of Lake Tahoe are awe-inspring, the fall colors can be extraordinary, and most of the trail is smooth and a treat to ride.

Heads Up!—This very popular trail is used by both hikers and bikers, and can be quite congested on weekends. Be especially cautious of hikers and follow the posted bike speed limits. The 4.5 mile Flume Trail portion of the trail, while well constructed, may be challenging to those who fear heights.

Getting There—Our trailhead is off of Highway 89, about 0.5 mile from the intersection of Highway89 and Highway 50. It is located in the Lake Tahoe Nevada State Park at Spooner Lake, about 27 miles from Tahoe City and 14 miles from South Lake Tahoe. A fee is required to park, with the proceeds going to maintain the trails.

Brief Trail Description—From the parking lot, head down a short hill to North Canyon Road, which you follow about four miles uphill to the saddle above Marlette Lake. You will find maps placed at several kiosks along the route. A 1-mile descent takes you to a junction next to Marlette Lake. Turn left and follow the road around the west side of the lake to Marlette Lake's dam. To the left of the dam, the Flume Trail begins as a steep single track which quickly crosses the lake's outlet creek. For the next 4.5 miles the trail traverses, mostly level, over the location of the former water flume that ran from Marlette Lake to Carson City. This flume carried logs in the late 1800s to build Virginia City silver mines. The lakeviews from the Flume Trail are spectacular. Eventually the trail reaches Tunnel Creek Road.

If you would like a shorter ride, turn left and head down this road to Highway 28. In the summertime you can pay for a shuttle back to your car. Call (775) 749-5349 or go to www.theflume-trail.com for shuttle information and times.

To continue on the Flume Trail/TRT loop, turn right and head up the steep hill 0.5 mile to the Tahoe Rim Trail, where you turn right. Follow the trail past Twin Lakes and begin climbing. The TRT heads mostly uphill for 2.4 miles, and then mostly downhill for 2.7 miles to a junction at Hobart Road. Turn right on Hobart Road and soon you will head downhill steeply to your junction next to Marlette Lake. Now you are retracing your route to the saddle above Marlette Lake and then on a long, fun downhill on North Canyon Road back to the trailhead.

Commemorative Emigrant Trail

Difficulty—Easy to moderately difficult. For most people who have experience on single-track trails, this is a fun and not-too-difficult ride. It is a special treat for advanced riders looking for an opportunity to ride fast.

Best Seasons—Late-May to November. The snow is usually melted off this trail earlier than any other single-track trail in the North Tahoe/Truckee area. After a mild winter you may be able to ride this trail by mid-April.

Highlights—This is a fun ride with gentle ascents and descents through an open forest that can be completed by strong riders in about 2 hours. While the scattered forest scenery on this hike is pleasant, the great riding conditions are what make it especially enjoyable. Keep your eyes open for deer, commonly found along this trail.

Heads Up!—Since in the spring this may be the only North Tahoe area mountain biking trail free from snow, it can be overcrowded, especially on weekends. As the snow melts and other trails become available, the number of riders on this trail will drop significantly. In the middle of the summer this very exposed and dry trail can be quite hot and dusty.

Getting There—Take Highway 89 about 4 miles north from the intersection of Interstate 80 and Highway 89 in Truckee. Just as you bridge Prosser Creek (the first large creek you pass heading north from Truckee), you will see a dirt parking area on the right side. Your trail starts here.

Brief Description—The trail heads 9 miles north through a recently logged forest, eventually reaching Stampede Reservoir, where you turn around and return the same way. The trail intersects with many dirt roads, but just follow the well-labeled single-track trail. Along the route you will see several meadows and Mount Rose in the distance through the trees.

CHAPTER 8

Resources and Amenities

Printed below are public agencies, Forest Service information centers, and other useful tidbits to help you plan your trip to the Tahoe Rim Trail.

National Forest,
Lake Tahoe Basin Management Unit
870 Emerald Bay Road
South Lake Tahoe, CA 96150
(530) 573-2600
www.r5.fed.us/ltbmu

National Forest,
El Dorado National Forest Information Center
3070 Camino Heights Drive
Camino, CA 95709
(530) 644-6048
www.r5.fs.fed.us/eldorado

National Forest,
Humboldt-Toiyabe National Forest
1536 South Carson Street
Carson City, NV 89701
(775) 882-2766
www.fs.fed.us/htnf

www.Tahoetrips.com
Information on guided excursions at Lake Tahoe.

www.Tahoeguide.com
General guide for a variety of Tahoe information.

www.Tahoe.com
Another all purpose web site, that includes the local newspapers.

www.flyline.com
Information on fishing in the Sierra Nevada.

www.tahoexc.org
Tahoe Cross Country Ski Area Website.

www.spoonerlake.com
Spooner Lake Cross Country Website.

www.theflumetrail.com
Flume Trail shuttle/Spooner Wilderness cabins information.

www.kirkwood.com
Information on Kirkwood Downhill and Cross-Country ski areas.

www.highsierra.com
An all purpose Lake Tahoe site.

www.tahoesites.com
An index of Lake Tahoe web sites.

National Forest, Tahoe National Forest
10342 Highway 89, North
Truckee, CA 96161
(530) 587-3558
www.r5.fs.fed.us/tahoe

Lake Tahoe Nevada State Park
P.O. Box 8867
Incline Village, NV 89452
(775) 831-0494
www.state.nv.us/stparks/lt

Tahoe Rim Trail Association
DWR Community Non-Profit Center
948 Incline Way
Incline Village, NV 89451
(775) 298-0012
info@tahoerimtrail.org / www.tahoerimtrail.org

Tom Harrison Maps
2 Falmouth Cove
San Rafael, CA 94901
(415) 456-7940
www.tomharrisonmaps.com

Useful Phone Numbers and Websites

Emergency	911
Tahoe Nordic Search and Rescue	(530) 581-4038
Placer County Sheriff	(530) 581-6300
El Dorado County Sheriff	(530) 573-3000
Nevada County Sheriff	(530) 582-7838
Washoe County Sheriff	(775) 832-4107

www.TimsTahoeAdventures.com
Information on hiking, biking, mountain biking,
cross-country skiing, and real estate at Lake Tahoe.

www.TahoeRimTrail.org
Official website of the Tahoe Rim Trail Association.

Afterword

Telling everyone about what the Tahoe Rim Trail has to offer is a joy to me. It is very satisfying to help others experience an incredible ridgetop view or the thrill of flying down a fun section of single-track trail. When I am guiding a trip and explaining about the beauty around us, it is invigorating and restorative. That said, when I go out for a mountain bike ride on one of my favorite sections of trail, I get a bit irritated to see all those other people out there as well. Who are all these people and why are they riding on this great trail that I used to have to myself? In writing this book, am I part of the problem? Am I fouling my own nest and the nest of others by telling everyone about the best places to go? Perhaps.

I hope that by providing the tools for people to enjoy their natural surroundings, I am increasing the understanding of how important it is that we protect the natural world. If you enjoyed this book and found it useful, please return the favor by doing what you can to protect what we still have and help restore what has been damaged or destroyed. Go to work maintaining a trail. Join the Tahoe Rim Trail, Sierra Club, or League to Save Lake Tahoe in an effort to keep this beautiful place as beautiful as it is now.

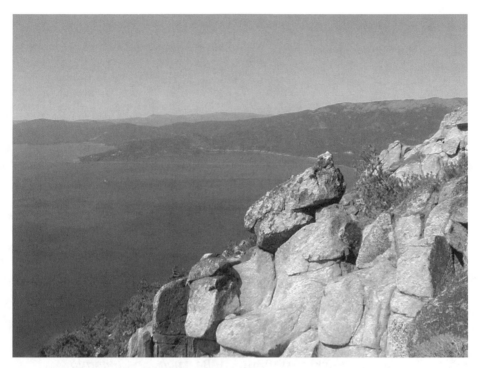

Send me your corrections or suggestions:

Hopefully you will see a revised edition of this book in a few years. Things are always changing out on the trail, so if you see something that has changed or is no longer correct in the book, please let me know and I will look into it for the next edition. Send me a note with your suggestions to: thauserman@telis.org or write to mail@wilderness-press.com.

Lake Tahoe from Christopher's Loop, looking north.

Recommended Reading

Audubon Society. *Field Guide to California*. New York, NY: Chanticleer Press, 1998.

Audubon Society. *The Audubon Society Pocket Guides: Familiar Mammals*. New York, NY: Alfred A. Knopf, Inc.,1988.

Backhurst, Paul, ed. *Backpacking California*. Berkeley, CA: Wilderness Press, 2001.

Blackwell, Laird R. *Wildflowers of the Tahoe Sierra*. Redmond, WA: Lone Pine Publishing, 1997.

Carville, Julie Stauffer. *Hiking Tahoe's Wildflower Trails,* Lone Pine edition. Redmond, WA: Lone Pine Publishing, 1997.

Cutter, Ralph. *Sierra Trout Guide*. Portland, OR: Frank Amato Press, 1991.

Graf, Michael. *Plants of the Tahoe Basin: Flowering Plants, Trees and Ferns*. Berkeley, CA: California Native Plant Society, University of California Press, 1999.

Huggins, Ellie. *What Shall We Do Tomorrow at Lake Tahoe?*, fifth edition. Truckee, CA: Coldstream Press, 2001.

Leopold, Aldo. *The Sand County Almanac*. New York, NY: Oxford University Press, 1949.

Peak Media. *The Trail Book, Lake Tahoe*. Hailey, Idaho: Peak Media, 1997.

McLaughlin, Mark. *Sierra Stories, The Tales of Tahoe,* Vol 2.. Carnelian Bay, CA: Mic Mac Publishing. 1998.

Miller, Millie. *Sierra Mountain Flowers.* Boulder, CO: Johnson Books, 1983.

Muir, John. *The Mountains of California.* New York, NY: Century Press, 1894.

Muir, John. *The Eight Wilderness Discovery Books.* Seattle: WA: The Mountaineers Press, 1992.

National Geographic Society's Field Guide to the Birds of North America. Washington, DC: National Geographic Society, 1983.

Schaffer, Jeffrey. *Desolation Wilderness and the South Lake Tahoe Basin.* Berkeley, CA: Wilderness Press, 1980.

Schaffer, Jeffrey. *The Tahoe Sierra,* 4th edition. Berkeley, CA: Wilderness Press, 1998.

Scott, Edward B. *The Saga of Lake Tahoe,* Vol. I. Pebble Beach, CA: Sierra-Tahoe Publishing, 1957.

Scott, Edward B. *The Saga of Lake Tahoe,* Vol II. Pebble Beach, CA: Sierra-Tahoe Publishing, 1973.

Weeden, Norman F., Ph.D. *A Sierra Nevada Flora,* 4th edition. Berkeley, CA: Wilderness Press, 1996.

White, Michael. *Snowshoe Trails of Tahoe.* Berkeley, CA: Wilderness Press, 1998.

Yesavage, Jerome. *Desolation Wilderness Fishing Guide.* Portland, OR: Frank Amato Press, 1994.

Maps

Harrison, Tom. "Lake Tahoe Recreation Map." San Rafael, CA: Tom Harrison Maps, 2000.

Wilderness Press. "Fallen Leaf Lake (Desolation Wilderness)." Berkeley, CA: Wilderness Press, 1996.

Mileages for the Tahoe Rim Trail

The mileages for the distances between points along the Tahoe Rim Trail are presented below. They are based on the cartographical work of the Tahoe Rim Trail Association, Jeffrey P. Schaffer, and Tom Harrison Maps.

Section Mileage Chart

Section Number	Location	Total Miles	Miles Between Points
Section 1	Tahoe City to Brockway Summit	19.2	
	Lava Rocks Viewpoint		*3.4*
	Cinder Cone		*4.1*
	Painted Rock		*7.0*
	Watson Lake		*12.5*
	Brockway Summit		*19.2*

(continued)

Section Mileage Chart *(continued)*

Section Number	Location	Total Miles	Miles Between Points
Section 2	Brockway Summit to Tahoe Meadows	18.9	
	Spur Trail to Viewpoint		*1.2*
	. . . .		*(Viewpoint, 1.5)*
	Road to Martis Peak		*4.3*
	Rock Pile Viewpoint		*6.8*
	Wilderness Boundary		*7.6*
	Rose Knob Peak/Gray Lake Junction		*9.8*
	Gray Lake Junction/Mud Lake		*11.2*
	Relay Peak		*14.6*
	Radio Tower		*15.0*
	Mt. Rose Trail Junction		*16.4*
	Mt. Rose Highway		*18.9*
Section 3	Tahoe Meadows to Spooner Summit	23.1	
	Tunnel Creek Road		*9.2*
	Twin Lakes		*9.5*
	Christopher's Loop Junction		*11.6*
	. . . .		*(Viewpoint, 12.8)*
	Marlette Peak Campground		*13.8*
	Hobart Road		*14.3*
	Marlette Lake via Hobart Road		*16.4*
	Spooner Lake via Hobart Road		*21.2*
	Snow Valley Peak Road		*17.2*
	Snow Valley Peak		*17.5*
	Spooner Summit Trailhead		*23.1*
Section 4	Spooner to Kingsbury	13.0	
	South Camp Peak		*6.0*
	Genoa Peak		*7.8*
	Kingsbury North Trailhead		*13.0*

(continued)

Section Mileage Chart (*continued*)

Section Number	Location	Total Miles	Miles Between Points
Section 5	Kingsbury to Big Meadow Trailhead	23.2	
	Mott Canyon Creek		*3.6*
	Monument Pass		*5.1*
	Star Lake		*8.8*
	Freel Peak Saddle		*10.7*
	Armstrong Pass		*13.7*
	Tucker Flat (Saxon Creek Trail)		*18.8*
	Grass Lake Junction		*21.2*
	Grass Lake Trailhead		*21.8*
	Big Meadow Trailhead		*23.2*
Section 6	Big Meadow Trailhead to Echo Lake	17.5	
	Big Meadow		*0.7*
	Dardanelles Lake Junction		*2.0*
	Dardanelles Lake		*3.4*
	Round Lake		*2.6*
	PCT/TRT Junction		*4.9*
	Showers Lake		*7.0*
	Sayles Canyon Trail		*10.5*
	Bryan Meadow		*11.4*
	Echo Summit		*15.3*
	Echo Lake		*17.5*

(continued)

Section Mileage Chart *(continued)*

Section Number	Location	Total Miles	Miles Between Points
Section 7	Echo Lake to Barker Pass	32.5	
	Upper Echo Lake Water Taxi		*2.5*
	Tamarack Lake		*3.6*
	Lake Aloha		*6.0*
	Junction with Mosquito Pass Trail		*7.4*
	Heather Lake		*7.9*
	Susie Lake		*9.0*
	Glen Alpine Springs Trail Junction		*9.7*
	Gilmore Lake		*10.7*
	Dicks Pass		*13.6*
	Junction to Bayview Trail		*15.3*
	Dicks Lake		*15.5*
	Fontanillis Lake		*16.0*
	Middle Velma Lake		*17.5*
	Phipps Peak Trail Junction		*23.1*
	Richardson Lake		*26.0*
	Miller Lake Jeep Road		*28.2*
	Barker Pass		*32.5*
Section 8	Barker Pass to Tahoe City	16.7	
	Twin Peaks Trail Junction		*4.8*
	Twin Peaks on TRT		*6.0*
	Junction of TRT/Stanford Rock Trail		*6.3*
	Ward Creek Road		*11.5*
	Tahoe City		*16.7*

Clockwise Mileage Chart

Location	Total Mileage	Distance Between Points	Counter-clockwise Mileage
Tahoe City North Trailhead	0.0	19.2	168.2
Brockway Summit Trailhead	19.2	18.9	149.0
Highway 431 Tahoe Meadows	38.1	0.4	130.1
Tahoe Meadows Trailhead	38.5	23.1	129.7
Spooner North Trailhead	61.6	—	106.6
Spooner South Trailhead	61.6	13.0	106.6
Kingsbury North Trailhead	74.6	3.4	93.6
Kingsbury South Trailhead	78.0	23.2	90.2
Big Meadow Trailhead	101.2	15.3	67.0
Echo Summit Trailhead	116.5	2.2	51.7
Echo Lake Trailhead	118.7	32.5	49.5
Barker Pass Trailhead	151.2	16.7	17.0
Tahoe City South Trailhead	167.9	0.3	0.3
Tahoe City North Trailhead	168.2	—	0.0

Tim's Top 5 Best Places on the Trail

For Views

Dicks Pass (Section 7)—Since it is quite a climb to reach the top, you'll want to spend some time enjoying the breathtaking views of two huge watersheds and a dozen lakes.

Christopher's Loop (Sections 3 and 4)—Located about halfway between Tahoe Meadows and Spooner Summit at the end of a short spur trail, it is not easy to reach this viewpoint, but you are rewarded with a view of of the entire lake and surrounding mountains (Section 3). The other great, east-shore lake view is from South Camp Peak, halfway between Spooner Summit and Kingsbury Grade (Section 4).

Granite Chief Wilderness between Barker Pass and Twin Peaks (Section 8)—Just south of the Pacific Crest Trail junction near Twin Peaks, at the end of a long climb, you reach a great open ridge, where you enter Granite Chief Wilderness. Views into the big valley of that wilderness, and toward Desolation Wilderness and Lake Tahoe, are spectacular. It's a perfect lunch spot.

Relay Peak (Section 2)—The high point of this ridge in the Mount Rose area is referred to as the "Million Dollar Mile" as it affords spectacular 360-degree views. On a clear day you can see the Sierra Buttes and Lassen Peak to your north.

Lake Aloha (Section 7)—On a midsummer day without much wind, while you lounge on a rock with one foot in the water, it's unbeatable to gaze up at the Crystal Range.

To Swim

Lake Aloha (Section 7)—Here is Lake Aloha again. What can I say? If you swim from island to island offshore when the water is warm, you will swear you have died and gone to heaven.

Middle Velma Lake (Section 7)—This is another great lake for swimming, with numerous islands just begging for you to jump in and swim to them. If you are northbound on the TRT, it will be over 80 miles before the next really good swimming lake (and that one is colder). Time for a dip?

Truckee River (Section 1 and Section 8 Intersection)—Even though you cross the river right in the middle of Tahoe City, jump in and float around; it feels great. If you're ready for a break, consider a leisurely raft down the Truckee River; contact Mountain Air Sports at (530) 583-5606 for more information. Also the Commons Beach on Lake Tahoe in the center of Tahoe City is about 0.25 mile east of the Truckee River on Highway 28.

Star Lake (Section 5)—At its very high elevation the lake is extremely brisk (OK, bone-chilling cold), but the views are great and Star is the best lake along the east-shore trail.

Showers Lake (Section 6)—There are these big, flat, granite rocks that go right down to the water's edge, which make for great swimming *au naturel.* Be prepared for very cold water.

To Ride a Bike

Painted Rock (Section 1)—Between Tahoe City and Brockway Summit, 2 miles in either direction of Painted Rock, is the smoothest, most enjoyable single-track trail you will ever ride. Your easiest access is from Dollar Hill at the Tahoe Cross Country Ski Area.

Tunnel Creek Road to Marlette Lake (Section 3)—This portion of trail can be used as part of a loop with the Flume Trail. It includes some tough climbs, and some thrilling downhills with spectacular views. Get off your bike to hike up to the view from Herlan Peak (aka Christopher's Loop).

Page Meadows (Section 8)—The Page Meadows area, which has an extensive network of trails besides the Tahoe Rim Trail, offers some wonderful twists and turns on very ridable terrain. Stay out of the meadow itself until it dries up in the late summer or fall.

Spooner South to South Camp Peak (Section 4)—This section offers great riding over sandy terrain with tremendous views along the way. Either turn around at the peak and enjoy the downhill stretch, or continue on to Kingsbury for something a little more challenging and technical.

Final Note—I can't tell you about that other secret spot. If you already know about it, don't tell anyone.

To Camp

Lake Aloha (Section 7)—Hundreds of great spots are available on this big lake. It will give you privacy when the smaller lakes are crowded.

Velma/Fontanillis/Dicks lakes (Section 7)—All of these give you the full Desolation Wilderness experience, however crowded they become in mid-summer. Very few campsites are available at Fontanillis.

Barker Pass (Section 8)—About 2.5 miles north of Barker Pass is a peaceful little meadow with great views, a stream, and a nice camping spot among the trees.

Star Lake (Section 5)—This lake is beautiful and the next is at least 17 miles away. Isn't it time to make camp?

Showers Lake (Section 6)—Showers is a beautiful little lake offering great swimming and fine views. If you go there in the middle of the week, it might even be quiet and peaceful.

Ways to Save Lake Tahoe

We have been blessed with a deep blue alpine lake surrounded by majestic mountains. We must make an effort to preserve this lake and its environment so that future generations can enjoy it as well. The Tahoe Regional Planning Agency has come up with ways to save Lake Tahoe. A few of the best are listed below. These are a good place to start, but don't hesitate to think up your own.

1. ***Take the bus. Share a ride. Take a hike. Ride a bike.*** When you pick up your car keys, stop to plan the trip you're about to make. Can you run several errands while you're out? Could you save this trip until you need to make another? Is there another way you could get there? Reducing the number of trips you make and getting around without getting in your car reduces traffic congestion, helps protect excellent air quality, and may improve your social skills and your health.

2. ***Fill . . . don't spill.*** If you fill it to the brim, gasoline may spill out of your tank and into Lake Tahoe.

3. ***Skip a stone and leave the other rocks alone.*** Rocks of all sizes and shapes are fish

habitat. Fish need rocks to carry out their life cycles. Underwater rock gardens are where they spawn, feed, and hide from predators. By moving or rearranging rocks you might destroy valuable habitat.

4. **Don't be a trail blazer.** Erosion from unmaintained dirt roads presents a serious water-quality challenge. Off-highway vehicles and dirt bikes contribute to erosion when they travel off the maintained roads. Kids, stay on the designated roads. Parents, make sure your kids stay on the designated roads.

5. **Take the beaten path.** The tread from hiking boots and mountain-bike tires are enough to cause erosion in the back country, so it's best to stay on the trail.

6. **You can lead a horse to water, but you shouldn't set up camp there.** The less activity there is in a stream environment zones, the better. The law requires that you pitch your tent no less than 200 feet from a body of water. That includes lakes, streams, creeks, reservoirs, and rivers.

7. **Garbage in/garbage out.** You could even pick up after a litterbug who went before you.

8. **Finally, teach your children well.**

The above information was provided as a courtesy of the Tahoe Regional Planning Agency. For more information, call them at (775) 588-4547.

Tahoe Rim Trail 165-Mile Club

The following people are official members of the Tahoe Rim Trail 165-Mile Club. They accomplished this by hiking or riding the entire Tahoe Rim Trail. Would you like to be listed in the next edition? Join the Tahoe Rim Trail Association and start hiking!

No.	Name	Year	No.	Name	Year
1	Steve Andersen	1998	20	Brenda Bowman-Giese	2000
2	Art Presser	1998	21	George Lovell Boggs	2000
3	Nancy Peach	1998	22	Clay Thomas	2000
4	Ted Peach	1998	23	Evan Thomas	2000
5	Dave Garner	1999	24	Nancy Devon	2000
6	Dave Migliore	1999	25	Helga Sable	2000
7	Rexanne Ring-Harris	1999	26	John Daegling	2000
8	Doyle Harris	1999	27	Alex Prodaniuk	2000
9	Bob Sumner	1999	28	Lauren Slominski	2000
10	Peter Leth	1999	29	Melinda Moon	2000
11	Tim Hauserman	1999	30	Joe Braninburg	2000
12	Terry Daniels	1999	31	Rob Richmond	2000
13	Marion Daniels	1999	32	Ron Weaver	2000
14	Allegra Willison	1999	33	Signa Hird	2000
15	W. David Brown	1999	34	Christine Weaver	2000
16	Fred Findeisen	1999	35	Shirley Moore	2000
17	Ray O'Neal	1999	36	Mike Stevens	2000
18	Andy Wertheim	2000	37	Barbara Remeczky	2000
19	David Giese	2000	38	Jan Corda	2000

No.	Name	Year	No.	Name	Year
39	Scott Hartsock	2001	78	Roberta Martinoni	2001
40	Bruce Eisner	2001	79	Lara Mullin	2001
41	Shannon Raborn	2001	80	Dan Power	2001
42	Steven Maskaly	2001	81	Thelma Reindollar	2001
43	Toni Blair	2001	82	Patricia Ann Robbins	2001
44	Timothy Luzzi	2001	83	Doris Stoessel	2001
45	Peggy Bourland-Madison	2001	84	Bob Byrne	2001
46	Jerry Brown	2001	85	William Staab	2001
47	Barb Cohen	2001	86	Susan Henson	2001
48	Deanne Hansen	2001	87	Carl Yates	2001
49	James Hansen	2001	88	George Churchill	2001
50	Heather Ross	2001	89	Ernie Baragar	2001
51	Carol Anne Velarde	2001	90	Maggie Olson	2001
52	Bob Lehman	2001	91	Don Fyfe	2001
53	Nancy Brisack	2001	92	Laurie Buffington	2001
54	Phil Brisack	2001	93	Nancy Dupont	2001
55	Susan De Voe	2001	94	Ken Powers	2001
56	Dave De Voe	2001	95	Marsha Powers	2001
57	Ming Shirahama	2001	96	Aaron Zanto	2001
58	Yvette Crespin	2001			
59	Paul Kofoed	2001			
60	Sara Holm	2001			
61	Mary Champers	2001			
62	Barbara Egbert Chambers	2001			
63	Gary Chambers	2001			
64	Derek Williams	2001			
65	Chip Kerby	2001			
66	Sandy Kerby	2001			
67	Jay Abdo	2001			
68	Linda Lou Williams	2001			
69	Tim Anaclerio	2001			
70	Bob Bankhead	2001			
71	Evelyn Denk	2001			
72	Brian Boggs	2001			
73	D. Brian Burghart	2001			
74	Johnnie Dyer	2001			
75	Karee Edwards	2001			
76	Ellen Goldsmith	2001			
77	Robert Jonas	2001			

Dogs

The dog version of the 165-Mile Club should be called the 500 Mile Club, since dogs always end up running at least three times the actual length of the trail as they chase squirrels. For regulations regarding dogs on the Tahoe Rim Trail, see pages 82-83.

No.	Name
1	Pele (Harris)
2	Beau (Harris)
3	Murphy (Thomas)
4	Pepper (Corda)
5	Marcel (Shirahama)
6	Tasha (Yates)

Index

For specific place names, trails and roads, see "Index to Place Names," and "Index to Trails and Roads" below.

Index to Trails and Roads

About the Author

Tim Hauserman has been a resident of North Lake Tahoe since 1960. He has hiked and biked in the area for many years and has been a guide for the Sierra Club, Tahoe Trips and Trails (a private excursion company), the North Tahoe Hiking Club, and the Tahoe Rim Trail. A member of the Tahoe Rim Trail Board of Directors since 1998, he became the 11th member of the Tahoe Rim Trail 150-Mile Club in 1999.

In his other life he sells real estate for Coldwell Banker Real Estate in Tahoe City and lives on the west shore with his wife Sandy and two children, Sarah and Hannah. Other interests include cross-country skiing, kayaking, and karate.

The Tahoe Rim Trail Association

Now that you've experienced the Tahoe Rim Trail firsthand, join us!

The Tahoe Rim Trail Association, founded in 1981, is a non-profit organization that relies on volunteer efforts to enhance and maintain this 165-mile trail.

Become a part of our trail crew, join the organization or make a donation and help us continue to make this a trail truly like no other.

For more information, visit the Tahoe Rim Trail Association website at www.tahoerimtrail.org.

Tracks at a Glance

7 in
hind

2¼ in
front

2 in
hind

Fox

front

BlackBear

Jackrabbit
(hopping)

rear

3½ in

Deer

front

2 in
hind
2½ in

Marmot

front

front

2½ in.

rear

Coyote

hind   front

Raccoon

2¼ in.

front

3in

3in

hind

Mountain Lion

front

1⅜in

hind

1⅞in

Bobcat

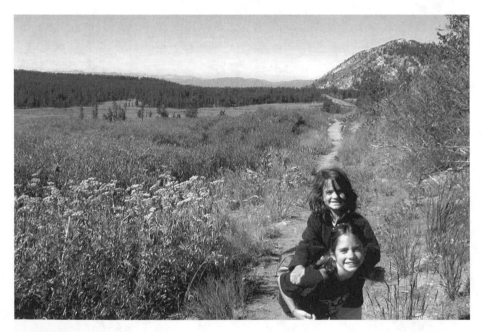

*Wild animals
on the trail
in Tahoe
Meadows.*